Informal Reading Diagnosis

Informal Reading Diagnosis

a *practical guide*
for the classroom teacher

THOMAS C. POTTER

GWENNETH RAE

California State University, Northridge

Prentice-Hall, Inc., *Englewood Cliffs, New Jersey*

372.4
P868

LB
1050
.P67

Library of Congress Cataloging in Publication Data

Potter, Thomas C
    Informal reading diagnosis.

    Bibliography: p.
    1. Reading Ability—Testing. 2. Educational tests
and measurements. I. Rae, Gwenneth, joint author.
II. Title.
LB1050.P67   372.4   72-4727
ISBN 0-13-464461-1
ISBN 0-13-464453-0 (pbk.)

Printed in the United States of America

10 9 8 7 6 5 4 3

Prentice-Hall International, Inc., *London*
Prentice-Hall of Australia, Pty. Ltd., *Sydney*
Prentice-Hall of Canada, Ltd., *Toronto*
Prentice-Hall of India Private Limited, *New Delhi*
Prentice-Hall of Japan, Inc., *Tokyo*

Contents

Preface   **ix**

1. Overview of Testing and the Diagnostic Process   **1**

Principles of Diagnosis   Types of Tests
Using Informal Tests   Administering Informal Tests
Development of Testing Programs

2. A Model of Reading   **6**

Sequence of Reading Skills   Categories of Reading Tests
Recording Methods   Concept of Levels

3. Perceptual Discrimination Skills   **12**

Auditory Discrimination   Visual Discrimination
Tactile Discrimination   Auditory Discrimination Test
Visual Discrimination Test
Tests of Visual and Auditory Memory
Tactile Discrimination Test   Learning Modalities Test
Summary

4. Receptive and Generative Language Skills   **37**

Echoic Language Skills Test   Generative Language Skills Test
Test on Following Directions
Listening Comprehension Tests   Summary

5. *Phonics and Word Analysis*   **56**

> Alphabet Recognition and Generation Test
> Letter-Sound Correspondence Tests
> Letter-Sound Generation Tests   Blending Test
> Syllabication Test   Structural Analysis of Words   Summary

6. *The Assessment of Oral Reading*   **91**

> Limitations of Oral Reading   Uses of Oral Reading
> Tests of Oral Reading
> San Diego Quick Assessment of Reading Ability
> Oral Reading Passages   Summary

7. *The Assessment of Silent Reading*   **104**

> Decoding and Silent Reading
> Silent Reading and Flexibility of Rate
> Silent Reading and the Study Skills
> Testing for Silent Reading Comprehension
> Silent Reading Paragraphs   Cloze Reading Tests   Summary

8. *Study and Reference Skills*   **117**

> Reading and Study Skills   Word Information Skills
> Literary Appreciation and Analysis   Scanning Test
> Word Information Tests   Information Location Tests
> Summary

9. *Attitudes and Appreciations
in Reading Skills Development*   **147**

> Testing Attitudes and Interests   Building Literary Appreciation
> Tests for Interpretation and Inferential Reading Skills
> Summary

10. *Teacher's Guide to the Use of
Informal Reading Inventories*   **169**

> Initiating the Reading Testing Program
> Suggested Groups of Tests   Flexibility of Testing Procedures
> Grouping for Test Administration
> Analyzing and Interpreting Test Results
> Construction of Informal Reading Inventories   Summary

Bibliography   **175**

Appendix 1   Tests   **179**

Appendix 2   Answer Sheets   **203**

Index   **217**

List of Informal Reading Tests in Book

Perceptual Discrimination Tests

Auditory Discrimination Test   Visual Discrimination Test
Tactile Discrimination Test

Memory Tests

Auditory Memory Test   Visual Memory Test

Learning Modalities Test

Oral Language Tests

Test of Listening and Repeating (Echoics)
Generative Language Skills Test   Test on Following Directions
Listening Comprehension Test

Decoding Tests

Alphabet Recognition Test   Alphabet Generation Test
Letter-Sound Correspondence Test
Letter-Sound Generation Test   Blending Test
Syllabication Test   Structural Analysis Test

Oral Reading Tests

San Diego Quick Assessment   Oral Reading Paragraphs

Silent Reading Tests

Silent Reading Paragraphs   Cloze Reading Tests

Study Skills Tests

Scanning Test   Alphabetizing Skills Test
Phonetic Dictionary Skills Test   Dictionary Definitions Test
Information Location Test

Attitude and Interest Survey

Literary Interpretation Tests

Word Analysis Test   Inferential Meanings Test

Ten to 15 percent of our adult population is functionally illiterate, according to the U.S. Office of Education. Seventy-five percent of the juvenile delinquents cannot read. These hard facts are stimulating a growing national concern with reading and reading problems.

The classroom teacher has long been aware of the vast needs in this area of the curriculum. Her concerns, however, are necessarily related to the day-to-day process of meeting the needs of her boys and girls. Gathering and utilizing information concerning her pupils' specific reading problems can be accomplished only if she is provided with specific assistance and guidelines.

The purpose of this volume is to provide a usable resource for student teachers and classroom teachers. The practical techniques and the instruments for reading diagnosis it presents are designed for those who wish initial and ongoing information on elementary school children of all ability levels and in all stages of development.

Current trends toward individualized teaching also create a need for thorough reading diagnosis. The child himself can give us much information vital to the accurate assessment of his strengths and weaknesses. This information is of central importance in planning his instructional program. Information on total class performance in specific reading areas can make flexible and purposeful grouping practices a reality. A continu-

ous system of evaluation may help the teacher to modify both the goals and the means of her teaching to meet the needs of her children more closely.

While this work offers an overview of the diagnostic process, it emphasizes specific informal testing techniques for use in the classroom. The tests may be utilized in an initial diagnosis of groups or individual children or for an ongoing evaluation of a reading program. The volume may also be a useful addition to the professional library of experienced teachers who wish to augment an existing collection of diagnostic tools and concepts.

In addition to presenting specific testing instruments, this book discusses the theory and practice of diagnostic teaching, describes the instruments and the rationale for their use, and offers specific guidance on administration and scoring.

Although there is an implied sequence of diagnostic procedures in this volume, we recognize that no single sequence of testing or diagnosis in reading has yet been shown to be superior to any other. Nevertheless, teachers may find that the use of a certain sequence provides continuity and consistency in meeting the unique needs of their children.

Many people have aided us in the preparation of this book. We would like to give special acknowledgment to Dr. Judith

Ramirez, University of California at Los Angeles, for her frank criticism and helpful comments. We would also like to thank our many colleagues for their support and forbearance during the preparation of this manuscript. More thanks go to our graduate students who field-tested the instruments in this volume. And we gratefully acknowledge the contribution of Dr. Ramon Ross, School of Education, San Diego State College and the International Reading Association, whose contributions to this work appear in the form of the San Diego Quick Assessment of Reading Ability.

Informal Reading Diagnosis

ONE

Overview of Testing
and the Diagnostic Process

Life in a complex and fast-paced society such as ours is often hectic and exasperating. Life within the classroom usually reflects the same complexity and demands much of both the teacher and her pupils. Classes are large. Children are varied in interests, needs, and abilities. And teachers are pressed to seek more and better ways to guide children in the learning process. These demands have led many educators to advocate increased individualization of instruction.

Many educators believe that as children progress through the elementary school, the degree to which teachers meet the needs of the individual child will usually determine the effectiveness of instruction in any subject area. The only meaningful classroom setting is that which reflects the interests and the works of the children who spend six or more hours each day within its walls.

It comes as no surprise that the larger the number of children within the classroom, the smaller the gains in skill and attitude development. As children are grouped into larger and larger sections, the span of interests and abilities increases geometrically. This inevitably results in lessening the immediacy and the continuity of instruction for the individual child in even the best instructional setting.

It is evident that not all children in a classroom need or can benefit from instruction in all phases of a skill or subject area at the same point in time. In fact, some children learn a substantial amount of material incidentally while other children need carefully structured experiences to acquire the same skills. One study showed that a large proportion of beginning third graders knew half the words they were to be taught in the basic readers of both the third and fourth grades. The child who develops many basic skills early in his academic career may find that much of what is subsequently taught is highly repetitive. Boredom is a deadly enemy in the classroom. While individualization of instruction cannot guarantee maximum progress for every child, it can provide more of an opportunity for the teacher to assist the child by establishing more efficient learning through appropriate instructional sequences.

Every child needs time and attention from the teacher. The more specific and direct the contact, the more learning is likely to take place. But this does not imply that group instruction should be banned from the classroom. Grouping certainly has a significant and proper place. When a group is formed for a specific purpose, and when it has been determined that the children do in fact need the skills and attitudes for which the group was formed, then group instruction becomes an effective and efficient means of teaching. Flexible grouping to meet specific needs is the key concept here.

Whether we are teaching on an individual or a group basis, we still must deal with two fundamental questions: What can the child already do in relation to a particular learning objective? What gaps in skills and attitudes does the child have that may prevent him from learning the task? The development of effective teaching strategies must be based on sound answers to those questions.

Diagnostic teaching is a direct attempt to answer these fundamental questions. Under this concept the teacher must be a diagnostician. She must gather information from all available sources—school records, the previous teacher, parents—and, most important, from direct, carefully recorded observations of the child. When this information is recorded in a usable way, then meaningful teaching can begin.

PRINCIPLES OF DIAGNOSIS

Diagnosing a child's past learning and present capabilities is a demanding task for any teacher. Yet it is a task that promises great rewards in increased teacher effectiveness and the best possible utilization of resources. The general principles of diagnosis are:

1. *Diagnostic testing is the basis for making curriculum decisions.* Gathering detailed information on an individual child is necessary for making these decisions regarding that child.

2. *No assumption should be made about the effectiveness of previous instruction or the child's retention of those lessons.* For example, just because a child is in the third grade we cannot assume that he has mastered the tasks traditionally taught in the first and second grades.

3. *Diagnosis must start with measurement of the more general abilities.* With this information, specific areas of difficulty can be selected for further testing. As more information is gathered in these specific areas, the teacher will be able to develop a suitable plan of instruction.

4. *Diagnosis is an ongoing process.* In areas where weaknesses are found, it is best to use diagnostic tests frequently to verify original test results and to determine changes in student abilities.

5. *Tests must be built from samples of the actual behavior being studied.* A teacher cannot know how well a child comprehends in silent reading from a test of oral reading comprehension. There is little evidence for transfer of knowledge or skill from one type of performance to another. Information gathered in an inaccurate manner will not lead to appropriate teaching strategies.

6. *The child must be informed of the nature of his problems.* Then he should be told why he should work in a certain way. This will encourage him to continue with a difficult task.

7. *A child should be rewarded for the effort he puts forth.* The teacher should not dwell on incorrect responses. A child deserves to be rewarded if he is trying to accomplish an assigned task regardless of the correctness of the responses. The child's efforts may be more closely related to his real abilities if he feels that he will receive approval or recognition for his efforts. This approach often reduces anxieties that many children show in a test situation. A feeling of defeat frequently accompanies repeated failure in any endeavor. This is particularly true of reading difficulty.

8. *Diagnostic procedures should be short.* In most skill areas it is more important to determine an individual's ability to perform a given task than to determine his stamina or fatigue rate. The short test is best for ensuring maximum attention to the problem at hand.

9. *Instructions for tasks should be clear.* Concise language ensures the child's understanding. If an individual's score on a test is low, it may be impossible to determine whether the result arises from a weakness in the skill tested or a misunderstanding of the instructions.

With these concepts in mind, we can explore the diagnostic process in more detail. The principal means of gathering specific information is a test of some kind. In a clinical setting an entire battery of intelligence and personality tests can be administered by trained people. In the classroom, however, a combination of standardized achievement tests and informal diagnostic tests are appropriate.

TYPES OF TESTS

Informal Diagnostic Tests

Informal tests are defined as non-standardized procedures for gathering specific information about a child. They provide data on the relative skill development level of the children at the time that the test is given. As such, informal tests give information on immediate learning objectives selected by the teacher. Their use provides specific information on each child. They are flexible and can be modified to meet a particular instructional need. They can be easy to administer and check.

The purposes of informal tests include:

1. Evaluating new programs.
2. Allowing comparisons of various groups to determine teaching or material effectiveness.
3. Determining progress in a particular activity.
4. Use as a screening device to determine which children may best profit from particular instructional plans.
5. Indicating an instructional sequence for a particular child.

Standardized Tests

Standardized tests have also been used to accomplish some or all of the above purposes. While there are many strengths in standardized instruments, their most outstanding are their general validity and reliability, their large group norms, their carefully developed administration procedures, and their efficient scoring procedures.

But these very strengths also contribute to the weaknesses of standardized instruments for classroom diagnosis. Frequently the group used to establish the norms for a particular test may not be comparable to the group to be tested. If the mean (or average) score of a group is at either end of the norming curve, the accuracy of the resulting standardized scores should particularly be questioned. Even more important, a test's power of discrimination is often crude and inaccurate if the scores are at the extremes of the original distribution. For example, if a group of children performs poorly on a particular test it may be because there were not enough questions, or items, at this level to ascertain its performance accurately.

A standardized test frequently depends less on specific tasks matched to classroom performance than on the ability to transfer learnings to new situations. Thus low scores may indicate poor ability in the skill being tested or poor transfer skills or both. This means that the teacher has little data on which to plan curriculum.

On occasion the teacher of a group is given only total scores from a particular test. While a number of children may attain the same result, they may have missed entirely different questions for entirely different reasons. Global scores give little information on which to base specific skills instruction.

The necessity for rigid adherence to specific procedures and time limits with standardized tests may cause confusion, particularly among young and inexperienced test takers. This lack of flexibility can cause children to fail a task on which, under more relaxed circumstances, they might have been able to succeed.

This constellation of weaknesses limits the usefulness of standardized tests in the day-to-day diagnostic procedures of the classroom teacher and makes a file of specific informal tests a highly valuable adjunct to teaching.

USING INFORMAL TESTS

Generally speaking, informal tests fall into two broad categories: individual tests, which are given on a one-to-one basis, and group tests, which are administered to more than one child at a time. Each type of test offers strengths and weaknesses for the classroom teacher.

Individual Tests

Whenever we work with a child on a one-to-one basis we can gather more information than when he is "lost" in the crowd. This is especially true when we are looking at reading behavior. During an oral reading test, for example, we can not only determine the reading level of the child but also record the kinds of reading error he makes. Is he guessing at words? Does he reverse words and say "ton" for "not"? Does he use only the initial consonant as his clue to the whole word? In addition, we can gather information about his attitudes and general level of performance. Is he tense? Does he act as if he were upset or afraid?

Information of this type can help us to select not only appropriate materials but also appropriate techniques such as the pacing of the child's lessons, the kinds of reassurance he needs, and the amount of pressure he can accommodate in order to do his best. When carefully recorded and analyzed, this kind of information can lead to many new insights for the teacher.

While some informal tests are designed to be given individually, many are given as group tests. Any group test can be administered individually, however, when more specific observations of the child's behavior during testing are desired.

The principal drawback to individual testing is the amount of teacher time it requires. Rarely will the rest of the class consent to disappear while a teacher works with one child. Thus the teacher finds it necessary to do a great deal of planning for independent activities when she wishes to do individual testing. Whether the additional information is worth the extra time and effort will depend on the needs of the child and the energy of the teacher.

Group Tests

Group testing can make it possible to gather great quantities of data in a relatively short period of time. Efficient scoring procedures can minimize correcting time, thereby making these tests both easy and economical to give.

Basically, the child can respond to visual or oral information. These inputs or some combination of the two can be used in both group and individual testing procedures. The types of responses will vary considerably with the kinds of abilities being tested. For example, the child's ability to comprehend spoken language can be measured by his written response; his demonstrational response, such as pointing to an object or holding up a card; or, in case of individual testing, his oral response. It is inadvisable to gather group test data from oral responses. Children will be influenced by other children's responses and will be distracted by the presence of the others.

ADMINISTERING INFORMAL TESTS

A child's responses in a test situation basically fall into two categories: recognition and production. In the first, the child is asked to identify the picture, letter, word, or word combination called for. In the latter, the child must generate the answer either orally or in writing. While the recognition response is in many respects an adequate means of identifying a child's strengths and weak-

nesses, the process of generating an answer will give considerably more information about the child's productive ability. This can aid the teacher in identifying the most effective methods and content for a particular individual.

A teacher can administer the same basic material in different ways. A phonics test can be given with pictures at one time, administered orally at another, and read and written silently at a third. These techniques allow individuals to demonstrate competence in a particular skill even though they may have a limited capacity to express ideas or communicate interests.

Varying the method of administration seems especially appropriate in light of some of the more recent research on individual learning styles. It seems probable that some children learn or respond better to visual stimuli than to oral stimuli while others learn in the opposite manner.

For any test, whether individual or group, the purposes of the test should be clear in the mind of both teacher and pupil. To yield the most accurate information possible, the student should feel a commitment to doing a good job. He will usually cooperate more fully if he understands that the test's purpose is to find the best ways to help him learn, not to assign him a particular grade on his report card.

DEVELOPMENT OF TESTING PROGRAMS

Initial Testing

At the beginning of each school year the teacher receives an inadequate profile of the individual's skills. In most instances data are at least three months old, and even this information may be inadequate for a sound diagnosis. Certainly all new children who have not been a part of a curriculum familiar to the teacher will need to be carefully examined. Initial tests may assess both oral and silent reading with the aim of establishing a general level of reading competence for each child. It must be emphasized, however, that this is by no means the end of the diagnostic process. As in standardized testing, two children may score at the same level in reading and yet have very different sets of skills contributing to that result. For example, two children may reach a reading score at the third grade level. But one may be very strong in word attack skills and relatively lacking in comprehension skills, perhaps because of deficiencies in background language experiences and the accompanying vocabulary development. The other child apparently at the same grade level may have highly developed comprehension skills but poor decoding skills. Because of this diversity of skills, additional testing may be desirable to ascertain particular strengths and weaknesses. Inventories that check various decoding skills, such as recognition of long and short vowel sounds, or tests for study or comprehension skills may be used depending on the functioning level and the needs of that particular group of children.

Data thus collected must be recorded in a meaningful and usable way. Class record sheets, group and individual check sheets, and individual reading profile sheets are highly useful for this purpose. Group records allow the teacher to get an overview of the skills and abilities of the class and make grouping for specific skills easier. Check sheets and individual profile sheets can then be made listing only those skills that need to be taught. These devices allow the teacher to plan meaningful and appropriate learning for her class. She may also use this sheet to keep track of progress for the group and the individual. Examples of record-keeping devices are included in chapter 2.

The initial testing period, then, provides the teacher with base line data from which to measure the effectiveness of her teaching as the year progresses. The retesting of the skills that are essential to satisfactory completion of the program will give her information on the growth of each child at key junctures.

Ongoing Testing

Teachers take for granted testing for retention of new material. Diagnosis is a continual process, however, and the teacher will find many times during the semester when retesting is appropriate. It is too often assumed that the child will remember a skill he has learned and utilize it two or three months later. As the teacher rechecks periodically she may find that she needs to reteach certain skills. Learning gaps are not unusual for any of us. Sometimes our attention wanders or we are absent on the wrong day. Children often feel frustrated when they recognize they are slipping behind and aren't quite certain where the problem lies.

New students naturally require the same type of testing that was used at the beginning of the semester. In areas of highly transient population, inventories can be put on tapes so that a youngster can be assessed with a minimum of disruption of the regular class schedule.

Testing may be necessary at other points because the child develops or the teacher recognizes a problem that was not evident before. If a particular child's performance takes a sudden dip the teacher will want to spend some time to discover the source of his problem. Often this process requires more specialized individual testing than the procedures used earlier.

Tests given at the end of the semester permit an assessment of group and individual gains. They also provide information on the general effectiveness of the teacher's program. An objective look at the year's accomplishments and failures can greatly aid the teacher in planning for personal growth.

Finally, the teacher will be able to provide data from such a testing program to administrators, supervisors, and others interested in the development of programs. These data are vitally necessary to the continued modification and evaluation of materials and techniques for effective teaching. All these purposes make diagnostic teaching an important tool for the classroom teacher.

The following chapters present and discuss the particular instruments in the repertory of informal diagnostic testing.

TWO

A Model of Reading

Experts in the reading field have developed elaborate models to explain the reading process. While these models have many implications for educational research, a simple view of the reading process is all we require for our purposes.

We will assume that the reading process starts with the reader seeing print. This neurophysiological process includes the reader's perception that this image is, in fact, something to be read, that the print has a purpose. The transformation of this image as perceived into sounds, either expressed or internalized, is the process of decoding. Whether the child recognizes the words "by sight"—that is, as a whole word he has memorized—or as separate sounds blended into a word, he is still utilizing a decoding process. The reader then attaches meanings to these words from both past experience and the context in which the words appear. He modifies the initial meanings he has grasped as he perceives surrounding meanings within the passage. Any particular reading act can thus be seen as the total process leading from the neurophysiological assimilation of print to the reader's thought processes and potential reactions to what has been read.

SEQUENCE OF READING SKILLS

It is well to remember, however, that the reading act, like any other process, comprises preceding skills and internal components that affect and even extend the act itself. Just as a child must scrawl in large strokes before he can develop the skill and dexterity to write his name, so must he master certain prereading skills before he can successfully become an independent reader. And just as the child prints before he can write his name in our more elaborate cursive style, so he masters some reading skills before others.

Below is an outline suggesting a possible sequence of these skills. While no research has shown conclusively that one sequence is superior to all others, it will be easier for us to look at specific skills from this frame of reference.

A. Prerequisite skills
1. Oral language development
2. Auditory discrimination
B. Beginning reading skills
1. Visual discrimination
2. Letter recognition and naming
3. Ordering skills
a. Left to right
b. Top-to-bottom patterning
4. Word discrimination
C. Phonics skills
1. Sound-symbol relationships
2. Blending
3. Syllabication

4. Structural analysis
D. Reading comprehension skills
   1. Word comprehension
   2. Sentence and paragraph comprehension
      a. Oral reading
      b. Silent reading
E. Study skills
   1. Locating information
   2. Scanning
   3. Rate of reading
F. Analysis and appreciation
   1. Synonyms and antonyms
   2. Inferential language
   3. Literary analysis

With this sequence in mind we can discuss the reading process in more detail. The child's earliest perceptions are merely noise, dark and light, hot and cold, comfort and discomfort. But at an early age he learns to discriminate meaningful noise such as the words his mother speaks to him when she is about to feed him from less meaningful noise such as a door being slammed. Thus the receptive faculty, the ability to distinguish and understand what is heard, develops before oral language skill.

Naturally the child's earliest oral expression is merely babbling, the crying, gurgling noises of the infant. Toward the end of the first year these sounds become words the parent can recognize. Labels for objects, people, and acts ("mommy," "car," "bye-bye") grow into sentences of increasing complexity as the child matures.

Reception and expression of the oral language are the child's first and, for several years, only means of communication; they are considered most critical in the development of reading skills. The basis for the child's processes of skill development are laid during these early years of language acquisition. We now have evidence that the variety and frequency of exposure to oral language together with the opportunity frequently to use expressive language is the paramount factor in the development of language processes.

When the child enters school and turns to the task of reading, the visual discrimination task becomes of key importance. Letter recognition and the ability to identify the relatively small differences between one letter and another are the key to this step in the sequence. Naming the letters of the alphabet is also an important part of the process of learning to differentiate one letter from another. The child who does not know the alphabet letters and their sounds is handicapped in acquiring methods for recognizing new words.

Of major importance in beginning reading are ordering skills, or skills of directionality. Left-to-right and top-to-bottom movements of the eye are quite significant in the development of reading patterns.

The child also needs to discern the basic units into which language is organized —the word. To understand that a word he hears or uses can be written down and that this particular sound pattern is represented by a group of symbols on a page is a major step in the reading process.

Acquisition of phonics skills, the relationships between specific sounds and specific symbols, must now be mastered. In phonetically regular languages this critical step is relatively easy. But in partially phonetic languages like English the association of different sounds with a particular letter and different letters with a particular sound makes mastery of the sound-symbol relationship more difficult.

Learning the sound-symbol association alone, however, is not sufficient to enable the child to decipher unfamiliar words. He must also be able to blend these sounds together into a recognizable word. Knowing common letter blends and regular sound patterns (blue, black, blend or pat, cat, hat) aids this process. Additional aids to independent word attack include the ability to divide words into syllables and the use of structural word analysis to distinguish prefixes, suffixes, and so on.

Simultaneous with the acquisition of phonics skills is the assignment of meaning to words encountered in print. Much of the initial meaning of these words is drawn from the child's background experiences in his environment. Virtually all the words that the child uses in his initial reading experiences are a part of his regular oral vocabulary and do not require him to master or even consider new meanings. Significant exceptions to this generalization are found among children whose regular speech is a nonstandard dialect as in certain areas of the South or in urban ghetto areas or who are learning English as a second language. For these children, the mastery of written English becomes a process of language orientation as well as reading acquisition. Such children therefore need enriched language instruction during this critical period.

Comprehension skills develop and mature as the child's reading vocabulary starts to exceed his speaking vocabulary. Now he encounters words in print that are not part of his speech. His understanding and use of context as a means of gaining understanding and depth grow and develop during this period. Sequencing of words and ideas becomes more complicated as sentences become paragraphs, paragraphs become stories, and stories become entire books to be read and understood. The child's comprehension skills must keep pace with the increased demand to read and make use of what he reads in other subject areas.

This need makes instruction in study skills a highly important adjunct to the reading process itself. The young reader must learn how to use books for a variety of purposes—to gather information, to generate ideas, to develop problem-solving skills, to experience the literature of mankind. This instruction can begin soon after the child learns to read his first words. These skills will prove of crucial importance as the child moves through upper elementary school and into high school, college, and the adult world.

Finally, the appreciation of literature as language becomes a part of the child's reading skills. Most children have the opportunity to learn about themselves and the world around them vicariously through print. Some children make inferences and gain insights into the subtler shades of meaning in which the printed word becomes much more than written speech and carries the reader far beyond the direct meanings of the words themselves.

This growth in the understanding of inferential meaning and the recognition of styles and approaches in literature is directly related to the amount of reading the child does. Just as success breeds success, so does constant and enthusiastic exposure to literature increase the child's desire to read and understand. Programs that include oral reading by the teacher and discussion and imitation of literary devices greatly increase the child's ability to understand reading and writing.

It is obvious that many elements of this continuum of reading skills overlap and complement one another. The continuum's separate strands are tightly woven together.

Some strands begin early, others later, but all contribute to the strength of the whole fabric and their full development makes it possible for the child to reach his optimal level as a reader.

CATEGORIES OF READING TESTS

There are three categories of tests that can be utilized in the reading area—general assessments, specific inventories, and individual skill tests. Each type of testing is appropriate for particular needs in the classroom. A general assessment is commonly used at the beginning of the year or with a late-entering child. When more information of a specific nature is desired, or where areas of weakness are noted, an inventory can be utilized. And when an area needs to be pinpointed a skill test of just the one dimension can be administered.

The general assessment asks certain broad questions about the child. For example, the ability to respond to language written down is a relatively general skill. A child's response to a paragraph giving specific information or directions can give the teacher some insight into his general reading skills. But if he has some difficulty, the general assessment does not tell the teacher the nature of the child's problem. Does he not know his basic sight vocabulary? Are his decoding skills weak? To find this out we turn to an inventory.

The specific inventory lets a teacher pursue hunches as to what the child's particular problem might be. For example, if he is able to pronounce a large number of words but does not appear to understand them, a comprehension inventory may be called for. This inventory may narrow the problem down to one or two areas of specific difficulty.

Now a skill test would be appropriate. For example, if synonyms and antonyms appeared to give the child difficulty during the comprehension inventory, he can be tested in more depth in this area to explore the degree of the difficulty. If he does not understand synonyms or antonyms he could be taught that concept and given appropriate practice. If he understands simple synonyms and antonyms but has problems with more advanced concepts or shows gaps in understanding, his instruction can be directed to those needs. This process of testing from the general to the specific can save time and energy in the classroom, since only the areas of particular weakness need to be pursued in depth for any particular child.

RECORDING METHODS

Whatever kinds of tests are administered, they will prove of little value unless the information they provide can be recorded in some usable fashion. Recording procedures are critical to the success of a diagnostic approach. These methods can be divided into three categories: profile sheets, check sheets, and case studies. Case studies are in-depth recording for one child and are usually the province of psychological or reading specialist clinics. They inquire into the child's background; the specifics of medical, psychological, and educational history; and specific data from various tests, including in-dividually administered intelligence tests and personality tests as well as various standardized and nonstandardized reading tests. While such studies are compiled in order to suggest the optimal use of instructional time and resources, the classroom teacher generally lacks both the training and the time to conduct them. For this reason we do not recommend a case study unless a teacher wishes to explore in depth a particular concern about a child.

Profile and check sheets, however, can be a great aid in recording informal testing information for both the individual child and the entire class. A cross sectional profile can be constructed for a single individual or a large reading group. In this way we can look at a number of skills for one child or one skill for a number of children to note particular areas of strength or weakness. Two examples follow:

Individual Profile Sheet

Name __John Jones__   Age ____   Grade ____   School _____

	Auditory Perception			Visual Perception		
	Level I	Level II	Level III	Level I	Level II	Level III
High	15	20	20	35	25	20
	(14)	19	19	(34)	(24)	(19)
	13	18	18	33	23	18
	12	(17)	17	32	22	17
Average	11	16	16	31	21	16
	10	15	(15)	30	20	15
	9	14	14	29	19	14
	8	13	13	28	18	13
	7	12	12	27	17	12
Low	6	11	11	26	16	11
	5	10	10	25	15	10
	4	9	9	24	14	9
		8	8	23	13	
		7		22	12	
		6		21	11	
				20		
				19		
				18		
				17		
				16		
				15		

Name	Auditory Perception									Visual Perception								
	Level I			Level II			Level III			Level I			Level II			Level III		
	H	A	L	H	A	L	H	A	L	H	A	L	H	A	L	H	A	L
John J.	✓			✓				✓		✓			✓			✓		
Sue M.	✓			✓			✓			✓			✓			✓		
Ann B.		✓		✓					✓	✓				✓				✓

Note that on the individual profile sheet different scores on different levels of the tests can indicate equally high performance. This feature is related to both the difficulty of the items and the number of items at each level. On the group profile sheet only the high, average, or low position is necessary to know, and this is all that is indicated. Such comparisons enable the teacher to give specific help only to those with a low rating.

Individual and group check sheets are used in much the same way, but they relate to more specific skill needs. For example:

Group Initial Consonant Check Sheet

✓ Knows item   O Needs work

	b	c	d	f	g	h	j	k	l	m	n	p	qu	r	s	t	v	w	y	z
Barbara L.	✓	✓	✓	✓	O	✓	O	✓	✓	✓	✓	✓	O	✓	✓	✓	✓	O	O	✓
Sally J.	✓	✓	✓	✓	✓	✓	✓	✓	✓	✓	✓	✓	✓	✓	✓	✓				
Bobby K.	✓	O	O	O	O	✓	O	O	O	✓										

This type of sheet enables the teacher to see the group needs in one operation. At this point, groups can be formed to teach the specific skills needed without repeating the instruction for those who have already learned it. An individual check sheet for a particular child would indicate a number of different phonics skill areas in much the same way.

Utilization of these kinds of recording device makes the teacher's job easier and more efficient. Examples in this section are hypothetical. However, profile and check sheets are included for the tests in each chapter. The choice of recording instruments will largely depend on the area being tested and the use to which the data will be put.

CONCEPT OF LEVELS

It should be obvious from the discussion of the sequence of reading skills and the nature of the testing and recording process that probably no two children will possess exactly the same skills at the same point in time. Because of this problem, it seems most appropriate to look at the functioning level of the child in relation to the total sequence of necessary reading skills rather than to assign an arbitrary grade level to his performance. Schools operate on a graded basis largely because of tradition and convenience. Grade designations, however, often tend to obscure rather than illuminate the functioning level of the child. As previously noted, the "third grade level" can indicate different profiles of performance for different children. A child may not have a particular skill at all, he may have it at a minimal level, or he may have mastered it well enough so that the teacher can dismiss it for her purposes.

For this reason all tests in this book are constructed on the basis of levels rather than grades. A particular test may have more than one level to indicate the level of competence in a skill or to assess the various components of a skill. The oral reading paragraphs, for example, comprise seven competence levels. Each successive level represents more difficult vocabulary, longer sentences, and more advanced ideational concepts. While these levels may seem to approximate the "official" grade designations, they merely indicate the child's actual functioning as a reader. Some children may operate on level IV or VI in a "first grade" classroom while other children who are officially placed in the fifth or sixth grade may function at level II.

Other tests in the book have different levels for the component parts of a skill. In the literary analysis tests in chapter 9, the word analysis test consists of three levels. One level tests for alliteration and word inference; another level tests for synonyms and antonyms; and the third level tests for synonyms and multiple meanings of words. A student may have mastered one or two of these components but not the others.

If the purpose of our testing is to enable us to teach the child what he needs to know beginning at the level and with the skills he already possesses, grade designations will be meaningless. With a functioning level concept we can concentrate on taking the child from where he is in reading as far as he can go.

THREE

Perceptual Discrimination Skills

The child's acquisition of language is a marvelous and complicated process. Through his interaction with his environment the young child builds his concepts of the world. He learns to attach labels to his surroundings and to use them to satisfy his needs. Most of this interaction, especially at the earlier stages, takes place by listening, looking, and touching. The child depends heavily on his perceptual abilities and steadily learns to refine and extend his discrimination.

As the time for beginning school and learning to read approaches, this ability to discriminate fine differences in auditory and visual stimuli becomes a vital part of the process of language development. In addition, it has been found that teaching methods that emphasize particular modalities—sight, sound, touch, or combinations of these—help some children to acquire this mastery more easily.

AUDITORY DISCRIMINATION

Auditory discrimination, the ability to differentiate sound, is the most important factor in the acquisition of language skills. In initial experiences with any language, the listener must learn to distinguish words that are different from others only in initial, middle, or ending sounds. Understanding depends on the listener's making clear and precise decisions about the differences in these sounds. The differentiation of words such as "bear" and "pear," "big" and "beg," and "bit" and "bid" is a challenge, and though some words differ only slightly, perceiving these differences is essential to the effectiveness of communication. A child who is unable to hear such fine differences in sound will have a difficult time with reading instruction, especially that which utilizes phonics methods.

Phonics instruction depends on the sound-symbol relationships of our language and the child's ability to associate correctly a sound with its corresponding graphic symbol. The child's ability to hear and discriminate the forty-four sounds of English are essential to his understanding of the written language.

VISUAL DISCRIMINATION

Similarly, visual discrimination aids the child in the acquisition of language and word meanings. Relatively minor differences in the child's environment, as he views it, have great impact on his life. The visual discrimination skills of relatively young children may make the difference between safety and

12

peril, as in crossing a busy intersection. Most differences in the visual environment of the child are very meaningful. At a very early age a baby learns to see, observe, and then associate meaning and appropriate language with what he sees.

Noting which way the arrow points on a one-way street is a rather obvious visual discrimination for the adult driver. Noting which word stands for "dad" rather than "bad" is a much more subtle discrimination for the beginning reader. The child who cannot discriminate between similar but non-identical shapes in letters or words has a difficult time learning to read. Testing for visual discrimination will help to identify children who make errors in discriminating shape, direction, and the total configuration of words.

TACTILE DISCRIMINATION

Tactile discrimination, the ability to differentiate stimuli that are perceived through the sense of touch, is perhaps the least developed of the three senses that may be useful in acquiring language facility. But many children do find enriched language meanings through the sense of touch. In addition, many children use their tactile sense as an aid in helping their other senses with difficult tasks. The child who reads with his finger under the words or needs to trace over a word before he can write or spell it is a common sight in the classroom. Helping children develop good tactile discrimination can aid in developing reading and retention skills.

Both the receptive and generative language abilities are affected by the child's sensory perception. Initial testing should be related to receptive skills, since well over half of all instruction depends on them.

AUDITORY DISCRIMINATION TEST

The auditory discrimination test, like all tests described in this volume, begins with items considered easy and appropriate for beginning elementary school children. At this first level, the child must determine if the two words or syllables pronounced by the teacher are "same" or "not same." All parts of this test include both nonsense and meaningful stimulus words. Nonsense syllables are used in order to eliminate any

possible meaning clues that the child might use to associate words and thus identify two synonyms as phonetically identical ("same") words. This is necessary to clarify in the child's mind that in this test it is only the sound of the word, not the meaning, that is "same" or "not same." As the teacher says the two words such as "rick" and "glick," the child writes or circles "yes" for same or "no" for not the same. Very young or immature children can respond by circling a happy face 😃 or a sad face 😠 to indicate discrimination. Such techniques avoid the possible confusion implicit in terms such as "same" and "different."

As the test progresses, the demand for more sophistication in auditory discrimination increases. This means that finer and finer discrimination needs to be made to complete the items satisfactorily.

In the second level of the test, the child is asked to determine if words sound exactly the same, partly the same, or not the same in any way. Some words in the test appear to be almost the same except for one sound. The six samples below show one example of each of the categories above for meaningful words and one for nonsense words. As elementary school children mature, the concept of middle, half way, or between seems to grow. But in the beginning years this is difficult for most children. The teacher must be careful in part 2 of the test to reread the directions as many times as necessary in order to clarify the concept of partly similar or almost alike.

Sample

Words Exactly the Same	Circle One		
rickshaw...rickshaw	Same	Partly Same	Not Same
sabco.....sabco	Same	Partly Same	Not Same

Words Similar	Circle One		
carpet......market	Same	Partly Same	Not Same
reccobale...reckant	Same	Partly Same	Not Same

Words Different			
north...father	Same	Partly Same	Not Same
glub....sak	Same	Partly Same	Not Same

In the third level of the auditory discrimination test, the child is asked to identify whether sound similarities between two words occur in beginning, medial (middle), or ending part of the word. This procedure gives the teacher a well-defined analysis of the child's facility to use the sound of the words he hears so she can determine not only his discrimination skills but also his ability to utilize word sounds in spelling tasks.

To make the nature of the auditory discrimination task as clear as possible, words that are different at the outset of the test are not only different in initial, medial, and final sounds but in number of syllables and accent pattern. As the test progresses, words with similar numbers of syllables and with similar accent patterns appear in the "different" pairs with higher and higher frequency. For example, if the test pair is "big" and "sit," the child needs to identify the middle sound as being the same in both words. This type of auditory discrimination is more difficult than the earlier levels of the test (see sample above) and reflects the maturing process of the child.

The principal question is not, "Does the child possess auditory discrimination?" but rather, "Are the child's auditory discrimination skills developed well enough for him to perform the tasks required of him at a particular level?" In beginning reading it may be sufficient for him to recognize that "ball" and "big" begin with the same sound, but as he progresses multisyllable words and fine discrimination in accent also become important. The third level of this test is designed to try these more mature abilities by including words that vary only slightly in prefix, suffix, and accent patterns. The test items are to be marked "B" for beginning sounds, "M" for middle, and "E" for ending.

In classroom use teachers will often find that they need to give only one or two of the levels of this test. Each test may be given and scored separately depending on the needs of the class. A general performance level of 90 percent on any level of the test should be considered satisfactory for that level. However, of much greater importance than the total score is the profile of the child's errors. Are middle or ending sounds the youngster's difficulty? Do differences in accent confuse him? Has he never learned to recognize rhyme? The answers to these questions can lead the teacher to offer very specific kinds of remedial help.

Levels for performance are meant to be general guides only. They are not to be considered norms, nor are they in any sense standardized data. They are provided to help the teacher determine whether or not the child needs additional testing or correctional help in the skills specified.

It is generally wise not to use this data as the basis for generalizing beyond the types of tasks included. Low auditory discrimination scores may have a relation to more serious problems; a child may have a hearing loss, for instance. But alternate and more specific evidence is needed to establish any causal relationship between such factors.

AUDITORY DISCRIMINATION TESTS

Directions to the teacher:

Read the instructions to the children clearly. Be sure that each child understands the difference between "same" and "not same." When reading the test items, pronounce each word clearly. Do not let the children see your lips as you pronounce the words, since this may confuse the purpose of the test by providing visual clues to the child. You can hide your lips by turning your head to the side or shielding your face with a sheet of paper.

When doing examples, draw a diagram on the board if necessary and walk around the class to be sure each child has followed directions. For children who cannot read the words "yes" and "no," the test answer sheet may show a smiling face in the place of "yes" and a frowning face in place of "no."

Proceed slowly through each item until the end of the test is reached or a drop in the children's attention suggests that a break is necessary. Test sessions for less mature children should not be more than ten to fifteen minutes in length.

Sample answer sheets:

Level I	Level I
Less mature children:	More mature Children:

Level I — Less mature children:

1. ☺ ☹
2. ☺ ☹
3. ☺ ☹
4. ☺ ☹

Level I — More mature Children:

1. yes   no
2. yes   no
3. yes   no
4. yes   no

Level II

1. same   partly same   not same
2. same   partly same   not same
3. etc.

Level III

1.	Beginning	Middle	End
1.	B	M	E
2.	B	M	E
3.	etc.		

The test items suggested are not intended to be either comprehensive or optimal in terms of differing classroom needs. Rather they represent a sample of a usable general format and items of generally appropriate ability level for the age-grade levels indicated. Each teacher is encouraged to modify the specific content of the tests whenever necessary to suit the vocabulary and other reading skills of her particular class. In most situations, however, the tests can be used in their present form and will provide the teacher with useful information on the instructional needs of her class.

AUDITORY DISCRIMINATION TEST   LEVEL I

Directions to the children:

Today we're going to play a listening game. Listen very carefully to the words I say. If they are the same you will circle the word "yes." If they are different you will circle the word "no." Let's try sample A. "gar—gar." Are they the same? Yes they are the same. So circle the word "yes" beside the A.

If the words I say are not the same, then you will circle "no" beside the number. Let's try another one, sample B: "rick—glick." Are they the same? No. Circle the word" "no" beside letter B. (Circulate and check that all children have followed directions.)

Samples

    A. gar — gar
    B. rĭck — glĭck

1. lўm — lўm
2. thăm — shăm
3. gōpile — gōpeēl
4. rĭf — rĭf
5. dĭs — dŏd
6. wăbmăl — wăbbăw
7. quĕpsŏd — quĕpsŏd
8. mōīne — mōīne

9. chōut — prōut
10. brŭd — brĭd
11. consonant — countenance
12. līre — tīre
13. quicksand — tricksand
14. happenstance — happenstance
15. different — diffidence

CHILD'S ANSWER SHEET (see page 205)

NAME _____

CHILD'S ANSWER SHEET

Name _____

A.	YES	NO
B.	YES	NO

1.	YES	NO
2.	YES	NO
3.	YES	NO
4.	YES	NO
5.	YES	NO
6.	YES	NO
7.	YES	NO
8.	YES	NO
9.	YES	NO
10.	YES	NO

11.	YES	NO
12.	YES	NO
13.	YES	NO
14.	YES	NO
15.	YES	NO

AUDITORY DISCRIMINATION TEST   LEVEL II

Directions to the children:

Today we're going to play a listening game. You will have to listen very carefully to do this correctly. I will say two words. Sometimes they will be exactly alike. Then you will circle the word "same" on your sheet. Sometimes they will be partly the same, that is, part of the word will stay the way I first said it and part of it will be different. Then you will circle "partly the same." Sometimes they will be completely different, and you will circle "not same." Let's try a few. Listen: "sabco—sabco." Are they the same, partly the same, or not the same? Right! Circle the word "same" on your sheet next to the *A.* Here's another one: "leego—leeho." Are they the same, partly the same, or not the same? Yes, circle "partly the same" next to *B,* because the first part of the word stays the same, but the second part changes. Try this one: "garp—patel." What did you hear? Right. They are completely different, so you will circle "not same" next to *C.* (Circulate to be sure all children do the samples correctly.) Now we're ready to begin.

Samples

A. săbcō — săbcō
B. lēēgō — lēēhō
C. gărp — pātĕl

1. mĭshbĕr — rĕssdō
2. dălbāin — dălbāin
3. sŭg — jănt
4. wĕckcōe — blĕckcōe
5. grēēpŭm — grēēpsŭm
6. wātion — wātion
7. plăd — fĭj
8. trŏb — flăt
9. chimney — chimney
10. blend — trend
11. recapitulate — recapitulate
12. final — finance
13. roughening — secondary

CHILD'S ANSWER SHEET

Name _____

A.	SAME	PARTLY SAME	NOT SAME
B.	SAME	PARTLY SAME	NOT SAME
C.	SAME	PARTLY SAME	NOT SAME

1.	SAME	PARTLY SAME	NOT SAME
2.	SAME	PARTLY SAME	NOT SAME
3.	SAME	PARTLY SAME	NOT SAME
4.	SAME	PARTLY SAME	NOT SAME
5.	SAME	PARTLY SAME	NOT SAME
6.	SAME	PARTLY SAME	NOT SAME
7.	SAME	PARTLY SAME	NOT SAME
8.	SAME	PARTLY SAME	NOT SAME
9.	SAME	PARTLY SAME	NOT SAME
10.	SAME	PARTLY SAME	NOT SAME
11.	SAME	PARTLY SAME	NOT SAME
12.	SAME	PARTLY SAME	NOT SAME
13.	SAME	PARTLY SAME	NOT SAME
14.	SAME	PARTLY SAME	NOT SAME
15.	SAME	PARTLY SAME	NOT SAME

AUDITORY DISCRIMINATION TEST   LEVEL III

Directions to the children:

Today we are going to do a listening exercise. I will say two words that are *partly* alike. They will be alike in the *beginning sound*, the *middle sound*, the *ending sound*. Listen very carefully. Decide which parts are the same. Let's do sample A. "bij—sil." How are they alike? Yes, the middle sound is the same, so you should circle the M to show it. Let's try sample B. "rekaped—rekaps." How are these words the same? The beginning sounds are the same, aren't they? So you should circle B for this answer. What letter would you circle if the end sound was the same? Good, let's begin. (Circulate to be sure all children do these samples correctly.)

Samples:

A.   bĭj — sĭl
B.   rekaped — rekaps

1. pĕntăl — bĕntăl
2. rĭftĭls — rĭftĭll
3. fĕutărd — fĕntŭrck
4. sĭntĭlon — sĭnpĭlot
5. cullington — cullingtail
6. sāilĕst — sāilĕsh
7. grensuster — grenkusper
8. perhāve′ — perhāge′
9. wallup — mallup
10. dălharĕst — dălmarĕst
11. thămĕss — thămĕst
12. kēberaff — sēberoff
13. clidĕrăl — clipĕrăl
14. tŭcking — dŭcking
15. suggested — suggestion

$\swarrow$ = has sufficient discrimination at this level

O = needs additional work

AUDITORY DISCRIMINATION CHECK SHEET

CHILD'S NAME	LEVEL I	LEVEL II	LEVEL III

Name _____

	BEGINNING	MIDDLE	END
A.	B	M	E
B.	B	M	E

	BEGINNING	MIDDLE	END
1.	B	M	E
2.	B	M	E
3.	B	M	E
4.	B	M	E
5.	B	M	E
6.	B	M	E
7.	B	M	E
8.	B	M	E
9.	B	M	E
10.	B	M	E
11.	B	M	E
12.	B	M	E
13.	B	M	**E**
14.	B	M	E
15.	B	M	E

VISUAL DISCRIMINATION TEST

Good visual discrimination is essential in the reading process, and so the next tests deal with this important area. The visual discrimination tests begin with items that are dramatically different from one another. Like the auditory discrimination tests, there are both letters and geometric forms (corresponding to the words and nonsense syllables of that test). All parts of the visual discrimination test are matching to sample items. In each problem, a figure, letter, or letter group is given first and a series of similar items appears to its right. Variables include size, shape, internal and external parts, and rotation. In addition, both simple and complex figures are included. Numerous examples of "same" items are utilized in some sets.

In level I, the child is asked on each line to mark the items that are the same as the sample. The dimensions tested are size, external shape, and rotation. Four items appear to the right of the sample and are marked "same" if they appear exactly the same. The initial items of the test, as shown in the examples below, are easily discriminable. Triangles are clearly different from circles or parallelograms, and O is different from a capital K or L.

Sample

Directions:

Circle the picture that is the same as the one in the box.

Gradually, discriminations become finer and finer so that the child must determine if an instance is the same or not the same in size and shape. In addition, particular items may be considered similar or not similar to the sample on the basis of components as well as entire figures.

In level II, the child is asked to identify differences in shape and line inside the figure as well as external portions. Each line now has four to six instances that may or may not be the same as the sample.

Level II also examines the dimension of rotation and multiple figure discrimination.

In level III, letters appear in the sample space in a particular order that must be identified as the same or different. The instances to be tested against the sample number four. The objective of level III is to determine the child's discriminative ability in cases that duplicate in many ways what the child encounters on the printed page. Entire words, meaningful or nonsense, consisting of three to twelve letters appear. The child must find components of the sample and find similarities in word configuration. He must avoid distractors that are rotated or reversed.

As with the auditory discrimination test, it may not be necessary to administer all levels of the visual tests to every class. Younger children may show meaningful results only on the first two levels. Older or more mature children will be able to utilize the higher levels. The names of children having difficulty with these tasks may be recorded in a class record sheet. Only children with marked difficulty will need further testing or remedial help.

VISUAL DISCRIMINATION TEST

Directions to the teacher:

In these tests the child's task is to circle the item in each row that is exactly the same as the first item. Directions to the child are minimal, but you will want to complete the samples with the children to make sure that they all understand the directions. At the start the first item in each row of the tests are placed in boxes to aid the child in identifying the correct object to match. This box is faded out as the test progresses. Items are designed to discover difficulties in recognition of external configuration, size constancy, rotation, reversal, and order. Each child will need an answer sheet.

LEVELS I AND II

Directions to the children:

Today we are going to do a task in which you have to have sharp eyes. In each row you are to circle the picture that is the same as the one in the box. Everyone look at A on your paper. Look at the shape in the box. Now find another one just like it in this row and circle it. (Check papers.) Good. Now try B by yourself. Now do all the rest of the page.

LEVEL III

Directions to the children:

In each row you are to circle the letters that are the same as those at the beginning. Try samples A and B and I will check them. Now do the whole page.

VISUAL DISCRIMINATION   LEVEL III   (see page 185)

	bp / mnm	bq / mnm	pd / mnm	bd / mnm	bp / mnm
A. / B.					
1.	gh	gn	ph	bh	gh
2.	ssb	bss	ssd	ssb	sbs
3.	sob	sbo	bos	sod	sob
4.	not	ton	not	hot	toh
5.	bad	bab	bad	bob	dad
6.	ursq	urqs	usrq	nrsq	ursq
7.	today	tobay	tadoy	dayto	today
8.	brwiltz	drwiltz	brwildz	brwiltz	brwiltz
9.	roughen	roughen	ruoghen	nouphen	roughon
10.	moisten	noisten	moistem	moisten	miosten
11.	dentally	dentaly	dentally	bentally	dentally
12.	beautiful	beautiful	deautiful	becutiful	beautiful
13.	lbingpiomy	lbingpiomy	ldingpiomy	lbingpiomy	lbinggiony
14.	discriminate	disoriminate	discriminate	discriminate	discriminate

The rationale for use of the visual discrimination tests is that they relate as closely as possible to the actual task the child faces in the reading process. In all tests described so far the child sees or hears the sample and the instances of "same" or "different" that follow. He may compare both and then check his initial responses. Thus the factor of memory is involved little or not at all. But to read, especially at an independent level, and to utilize phonics teaching, he must be able to remember a visual and/or auditory pattern. The child who just can't seem to remember "that word" has a difficult time acquiring basic sight vocabulary or attacking new words in a decoding process. Some simple tests of auditory and visual memory can help the teacher find those youngsters who need additional training in these areas.

Auditory and visual memory tests are organized from simple to complex. At first they present the child with the same dimensions as those of the nonmemory tests. In visual discrimination, for example, the child is asked to make decisions on external shape and size. But now the items are presented on flash cards by the teacher. The time is carefully controlled by the teacher.

In the visual memory test, the task is to retain an image viewed for three to six seconds. The child is presented items that differ in external configuration, size, rotation, or order or may be reversed. Both geometric shapes and meaningful words are presented, and the difficulty of the material gradually increases. Six second counts are allowed on the last three items to provide adequate viewing time for the long words involved.

In the auditory memory test, level I is devoted to words that vary from same to greatly different. The child hears the two words to be compared at intervals of five and ten seconds. He simply indicates "same" for the two utterances.

In level II, the task is to compare sentences that may be the same or may differ in varying degrees. In this part, the task is to remember the sample over a period of five or ten seconds. Here the child must decide whether the sentences are "same" or "not same." The child here must apply auditory discrimination on a broader scale than he has for words and wordlike utterances. If a

child has had difficulty with the visual or auditory discrimination test he should not be given the corresponding memory test, since this is a higher-level skill. A check sheet similar to those for auditory and visual discrimination will be appropriate for these tests.

VISUAL MEMORY TEST

Directions to the teacher:

To administer this test it is necessary for you to make twenty-two large cards displaying the items to be remembered. The child's task is to look at the card, and then, from memory, circle the correct item on his test sheet. The items test for external configuration, rotation, reversal, order, and whole word, as in the visual discrimination test, with the added factor of memory. Cards should be held up for approximately three seconds (slow silent count of three). Go through the samples with the children, making sure that they do not circle on the sheet until after the card is put down. Make sure the cards are held in the correct direction.

$\checkmark$ = has sufficient discrimination at this level

O = needs additional work

VISUAL DISCRIMINATION CHECK SHEET

CHILD'S NAME	LEVEL I	LEVEL II	LEVEL III

Teacher cards:

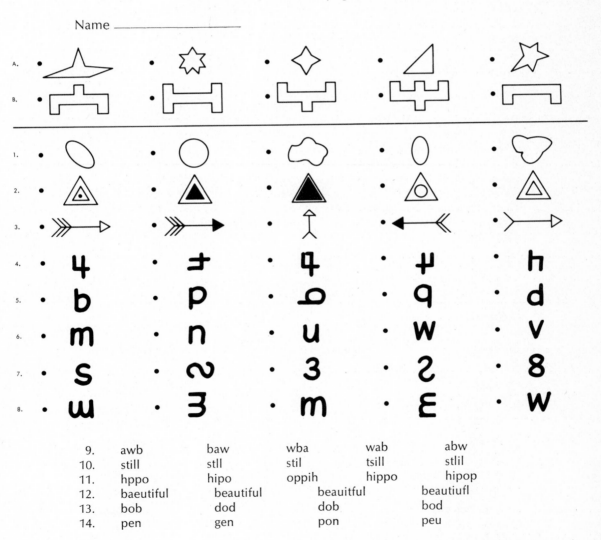

A. B. 1. 2. 3. 4. 4
5. d   6. u   7. 3   8. m   9. wab   10. still   11. hippo
12. beautiful   13. bod   14. pen   15. running   16. ballingry
17. populate   18. strodbecker   19. consternation   20. stipulate

Directions to the children:

Today we're going to play a memory game. I will hold up some cards and you are to look at the cards for as long as I hold it. When I put the card down put a circle around the picture or word that looks exactly like the one on the card. Do not circle *anything* until I put the card down. Let's try sample A. Look at the card carefully. (Count to three silently.) Now circle the same picture. (Check answers.) Now do sample B. (Hold up card, count to three silently.) Did everyone circle this? (Check.) Now we can begin. (Show last three items for count of six.)

VISUAL MEMORY (see pages 187-188)

Name _____

9.	awb	baw	wba	wab	abw
10.	still	stll	stil	tsill	stlil
11.	hppo	hipo	oppih	hippo	hipop
12.	baeutiful	beautiful	beauitful	beautiufl	
13.	bob	dod	dob	bod	
14.	pen	gen	pon	peu	

15.	nurring	running	runniug	rnuuing
16.	ballingry	balinpry	bolingry	ballinger
17.	populate	podubate	popalete	poplte
18.	straddecker	strodbecker	strobdek	srodbecker
19.	reservation	conservation	consternation	concerning
20.	stimulate	stipulate	scintillate	sintilap

AUDITORY MEMORY TEST   LEVEL I

Directions to the teacher:

In this test you are to pronounce the word or sentence in column 1 and then, after a pause, pronounce the word or sentence in column 2. Each level is divided into two sections. The first section requires a pause of five seconds between the words in column 1 and column 2, and the second section requires a pause of ten seconds between columns. The child's task is to circle "same" or "not same" for each pair. The pupil response sheet indicating happy and sad faces may be used for young or immature children. Speak clearly, but do not stress syllables of words or particular words in sentences. Check to be sure all children can do sample items.

Directions to the children:

Today you are going to need to be good listeners. I am going to say a word, then I will stop and wait for a short while. Then I will say the same word or a different word. You must remember what I said the first time and then decide if the next thing I say is the same or not the same as the first. If the word is the same both times, you will circle the word "same" (*or* the happy face) on your answer sheet. If the word is not the same you will circle "not same" (*or* the sad face). Let's try sample A. "Eat" (pause five seconds), "kit." Were they the same or not the same? (Check each paper.) Let's try sample B. "Play" (pause ten seconds), "play." Were they the same or different? (Check each paper.) Now we'll start.

LEVEL I

Section A

COLUMN 1	(pause five seconds)	COLUMN 2
1. rift		1. gift
2. jump		2. jumped
3. running		3. funning
4. batch		4. batch
5. bag		5. beg
6. burst		6. burst
7. fragile		7. frog pile
8. interior		8. exterior
9. presuppose		9. predispose
10. truncated		10. truncated

Section B

COLUMN 1	(pause ten seconds)	COLUMN 2
1. tisket		1. tasket
2. uncarbonated		2. uncarbonater
3. recirculating		3. recalculating
4. rudimentary		4. rudimentary
5. expectation		5. expectator
6. indicated		6. indicated
7. argumentative		7. argumentation
8. beautiful		8. beautifully
9. rasculate		9. resculate
10. reticular		10. redicular
11. pregistator		11. pregistator
12. memorize		12. memorized
13. bibliography		13. bibliotherapy
14. modernize		14. modernize
15. practication		15. dractication

CHILD'S ANSWER SHEET   LEVEL I

Section A

1.	SAME	NOT SAME
2.	SAME	NOT SAME
3.	SAME	NOT SAME
4.	SAME	NOT SAME
5.	SAME	NOT SAME
6.	SAME	NOT SAME
7.	SAME	NOT SAME
8.	SAME	NOT SAME
9.	SAME	NOT SAME
10.	SAME	NOT SAME

Section B

1.	SAME	NOT SAME
2.	SAME	NOT SAME
3.	SAME	NOT SAME
4.	SAME	NOT SAME
5.	SAME	NOT SAME
6.	SAME	NOT SAME
7.	SAME	NOT SAME
8.	SAME	NOT SAME
9.	SAME	NOT SAME
10.	SAME	NOT SAME
11.	SAME	NOT SAME
12.	SAME	NOT SAME
13.	SAME	NOT SAME
14.	SAME	NOT SAME
15.	SAME	NOT SAME

Directions to the teacher:

In this test you are to pronounce the sentence in column 1, and then, after a pause, pronounce the sentence in column 2. Each level is divided into two sections. The first section requires a pause of five seconds between the sentences in columns 1 and 2, and the second section requires a ten-second pause between columns. The child's task is to circle "same" or "not same" for each pair. The pupil response sheet indicating happy and sad faces may be used for young or immature children. Speak clearly but do not stress syllables of words or particular words in sentences. Check to be sure all children can do sample items.

Directions to the children:

Today you are going to need to be good listeners. I am going to say a sentence, then I will stop and wait for a short while. Then I will say the same sentence or a different sentence. You must remember what I said the first time and then decide if the next thing I say is the same or not the same as the first. If the sentence is the same both times, you will circle the word "same" (*or* the happy face) on your answer sheet. If the sentence is not the same you will circle "not same" (*or* the sad face). Let's try sample *A*. "Bill and Sally are running." (Pause five seconds.) "Bill and Sally were running." Were they the same or not the same? (Check.) Let's try sample *B*. "Come and look at me." (Pause ten seconds.) "Come and look at me." Were they the same or different? (Check.) Now we'll start.

LEVEL II

Section A

(pause five seconds)

COLUMN 1	COLUMN 2
1. Will you stop please.	1. Will you stop please.
2. Come into the house.	2. Come into the horse.
3. Can you see the man.	3. Can't you see the man.
4. I will come home soon.	4. I will come home soon.
5. When will dinner be ready.	5. When will dinner be ready.
6. When the car stops, you can get out.	6. When the cart starts, you can get on.
7. Once upon a time, the story started.	7. Once upon a time, the story started.
8. We will go shopping soon.	8. We will not go shopping soon.
9. The beautiful magician waved her wonderful wand.	9. The beautiful magician wove her wonderful wand.
10. Jumping gracefully the gazelle cleared the hurdle.	10. Jumping gratefully the gazelle cleaned the huddle.

Section B

(pause ten seconds)

COLUMN 1	COLUMN 2
1. Welcome to my igloo, said the eskimo.	1. Welcome to my igloo, said the eskimo.

2. When will the daffodils bloom in the spring.
3. Streamers and balloons flew gaily at the gala party.
4. Winter is the season for whirling, twirling snowflakes.
5. Jump into my catamaran and we will cruise the Pacific.
6. For your edification the concert was magnificent.
7. Roses, violets, and chrysanthemums bloomed profusely in the garden.
8. Ponies, goats, and horses ate the oats, hay, and alfalfa.
9. John, Tim, Sally, and Barbara row and raced through the grass.
10. Reluctant quadrupeds masticated contentedly on the verdant foliage.

2. When will the dandelions blossom in the spring.
3. Streamers and balloons flew gladly at the gaily party.
4. Winter is the reason for twirling, swirling snowflakes.
5. Jump into my counterland and we will comb the Terrific.
6. For you pontification the concept was magnified.
7. Roses, violets, and chrysanthemums bloomed profusely in the garden.
8. Ponies, horses, and goats ate the hay, alfalfa, and oats.
9. John, Tim, Barbara, and Sally rowed and ran through the grass.
10. Reluctant quadrupeds masticated constantly on the virgin foliage.

TACTILE DISCRIMINATION TEST

Psychologists tell us that the sense of touch is a vital part of our developmental experiences. Particularly in the very early years of our lives, touching everything in our environment is seemingly as necessary as seeing it. Many parents will attest to the fact that at the age of six to fourteen months, everything that a baby can reach goes into his mouth. Unfortunately, in later periods of childhood and as adults a visit to places filled with interesting or unusual objects almost always includes verbal or written warnings, "Don't touch." Though our culture has a fetish about not touching many things in our environment, some children in the elementary years do learn at an accelerated pace if allowed or encouraged to touch, trace, or otherwise interact tactilely with the pictures and print they encounter.

To determine the child's adeptness at tactile discrimination, an informal test utilizing cards with raised areas or objects can be administered. In the tactile discrimination test, children's ability to determine shape and size by touching without seeing is explored together with a test to determine their ability to tell the number of items presented. In the first level of the test the child is asked to determine whether one item is bigger or smaller than another, whether it is round or flat-sided, and if it has a hollow in the center "like a doughnut" or not. In the second level, the child decides on the number of objects he feels on the cards and tells whether the objects are the same or different in shape.

A third level deals with identities in which the child determines both the number and shape of the objects. In the final part of the test, he is asked to recognize letters and words that he can feel when his view of the words and letters is obstructed.

TEST OF TACTILE DISCRIMINATION

Directions to the teacher:

This is a specialized test that must be given on a one-to-one basis. The materials used are simple to make but must be prepared in advance. The test is meant to be administered to children who have shown difficulty in earlier tests with problems such as inability to discriminate likenesses and differences or tendencies to reverse and rotate. The information gained, however, can be beneficial for any child. Methods that employ a tactile approach (that is, tracing words or sandpaper letters) are often advantageous with children. This test attempts to help the teacher pinpoint areas of strength and weakness in tactile discrimination. Materials needed:

1. A "blind box" with a three inch hole in one end for the child to put his hand in and a five inch slot in the other end for a card. The hole must be large enough for the child to move his hand around easily. A shoebox is the proper size.
2. Five-by-eight-inch index cards or heavier chipboard for cards.
3. White glue and salt to make figures on cards.

Notice that one side of the card is labeled "T" and should always be the side closest to the teacher when placed in he box. In this test start all children at level I.

Directions to the children:

Today we're going to play a card touching game. Look at this card (show sample). This side is mine (point to it) and this side is yours. Close your eyes and feel the card. Is my side bigger or smaller than yours? (If the child does not understand the bigger-smaller concept, ask him, "Which one is big, mine or yours?" Guide his hand if necessary, saying "mine, yours.") Now I'm going to put this same card in the box. You put your hand in this open part of the box (demonstrate). Remember, my side is in the back of the box and your side is near the front by the hole. Now tell me if mine is bigger or smaller. (Work with this card until child understands the task.) Now I will put these cards (show five cards) in the box one at a time. Each time you will tell me if my side is bigger or smaller than yours.

LEVEL I

1. Is mine bigger or smaller than yours?

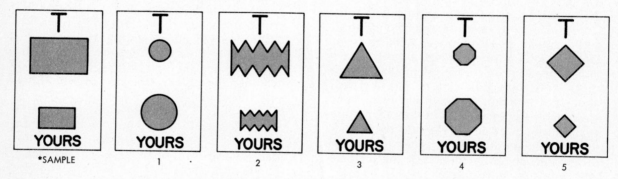

2. Look at this sample. Feel the shapes. Is mine or yours rounded?

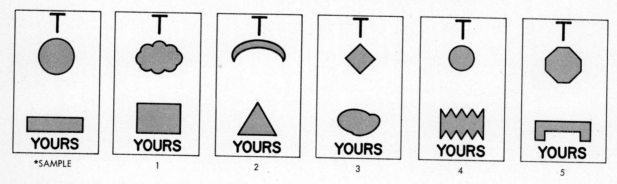

3. Now, one of these shapes has a hollow center like a doughnut. (Put in box without child touching.) Does mine or yours have a hollow center?

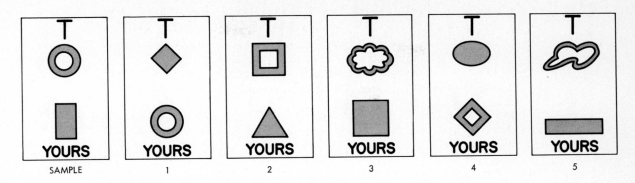

Note: The teacher may want to stop at this point and continue testing at a later time.

LEVEL II

If the test was discontinued before this level was begun, remind the child how the game was played.

1. On these cards you are going to see which side has more shapes on it, mine or yours.

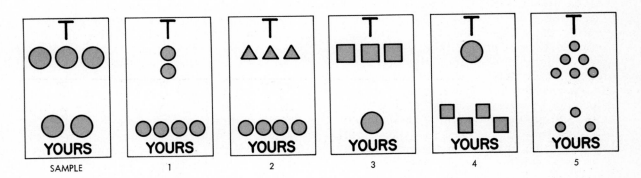

2. How many shapes are there on each card?

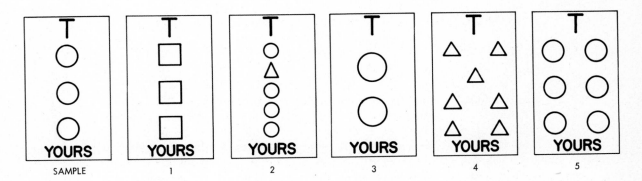

Note: The teacher may want to make cards for other numbers as well.

Name the letter that you feel in the box.

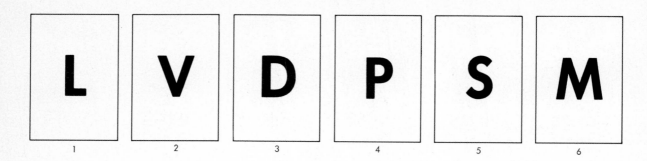

1   2   3   4   5   6

Note: This level should only be used for children who already know their letter names. Cards for other letters may also be made and used. These cards are also useful for a training program that includes tracing letter names.

LEARNING MODALITIES TEST

Many authors and educators apparently assume that children generally learn better by hearing than by viewing something and that one or more auditory and visual exposures to a particular idea is the best or most appropriate way to learn. These assumptions often lead to an educational presentation that relies on talking with an occasional picture thrown in. At later stages in the educational process the "talk" is all written down in books and the visual presentation is in the form of pictures on a page. But some research indicates that some children learn very slowly, if at all, through traditional auditory-visual presentation techniques.

In what ways does a given child learn best? Does he need to hear and see things at the same time? Does he learn better if he can also touch and trace? Does he need all of these modes of presentation, or is just one sufficient? To give the teacher clues to help answer these questions, an informal test of acquisition of and response to words and phrases in different sense modalities is provided. The test includes only presentation and response sequences. Equivalent but not identical material is presented in visual modes only or with simultaneous auditory presentation. For the visual mode only, for example, the child may be shown a word and picture printed on a card and then be required to recognize the word after a thirty-second delay. In auditory-with-visual presentation the child may be shown a word and told what the word is, then be asked to recognize it as before. At the earliest levels of the test, the child may respond orally rather than on paper.

LEARNING MODALITIES TEST

Directions to the teacher:

This test must be administered individually with a set of cards made in advance. Different sections of the test may be administered at different times at the convenience of the teacher. The first section requires the child to utilize the visual learning modality, the second section looks at auditory learning, and the third uses a combination of these two modes of learning. These tests are especially useful in determining which learning approach is best for the child. The child responds verbally, either "yes" or "no," to each question. A dummy card is shown between each set of two cards and can be the same in all instances.

Directions to the children: Part 1

Look at this card. (Show card 1.) This is its name. (Point to the word, pause twenty seconds.) Now look at this card. (Show dummy card five seconds; now show card 1A.) Is this the right name for the picture? (Do this for each set of cards.)

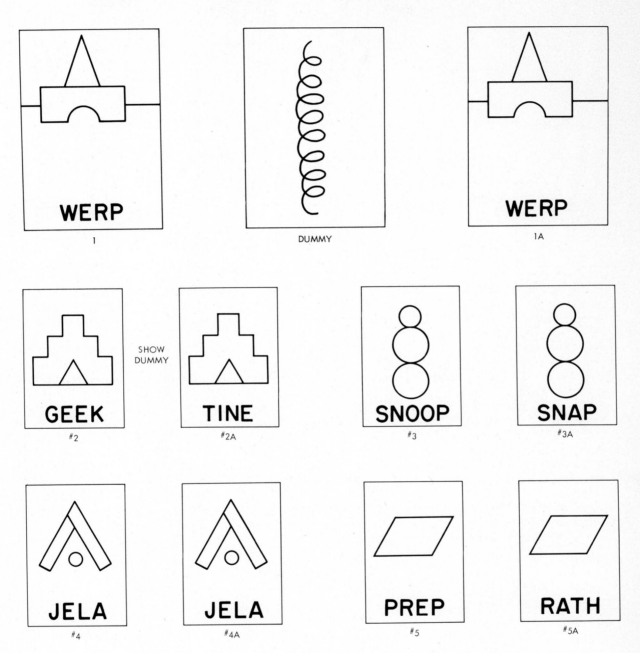

Directions to the children: Part 2

Look at this picture of a "wath." (Show card 1; pause twenty seconds.) Now look at this card. (Show dummy card for five seconds; show card 1A.) Is this a wath? (Do this for each set of cards.)

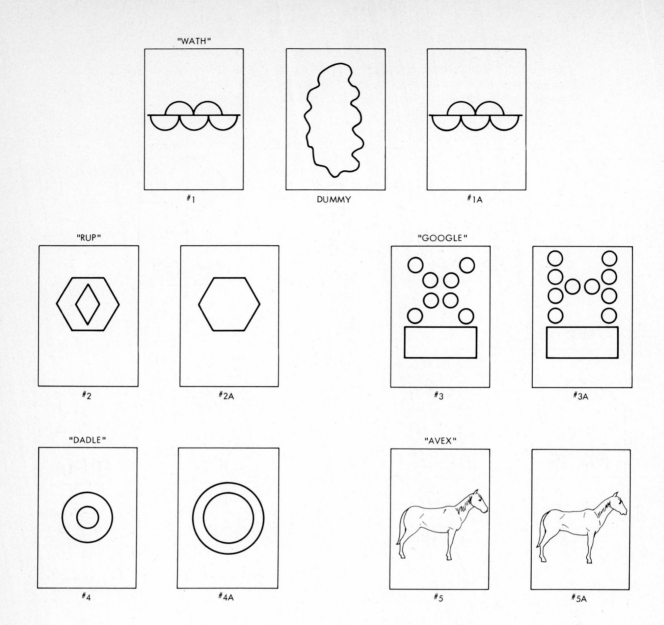

Directions to the child: Part 3

Look at this picture of a "shoop." (Show card 1; pause twenty seconds.) Now look at this card. (Show dummy card for 5 seconds; show card 1A.) Is this a shoop? (Do this for each set of cards.)

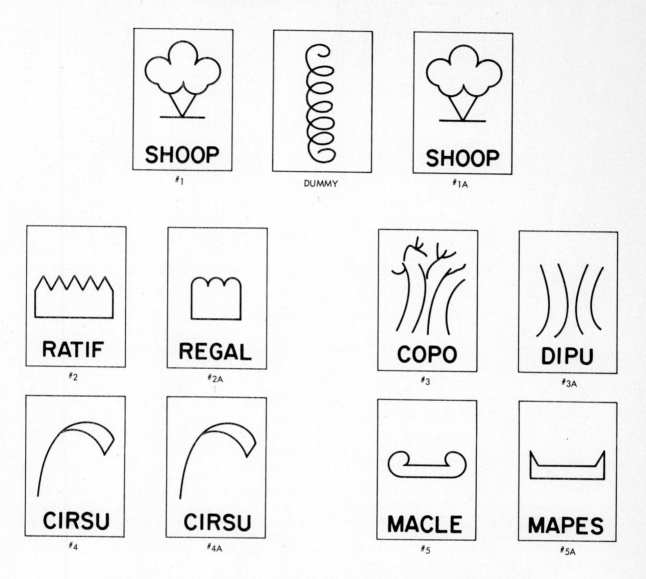

Note: The number of items in any section may be increased as needed. Some more immature children may need work with additional cards.

CHILD'S NAME _____   AGE _____

Date Tested							
Test							
Auditory Discrimination							
Level I							
Level II							
Level III							
Visual Discrimination							
Level I							
Level II							
Level III							
Visual Memory Test							
Auditory Memory Test							
Level I							
Level II							
Tactile Discrimination Test							
Level I							
Level II							
Level III							
Learning Modalities Test							

$\sqrt{}$ = Has sufficient discrimination at this level
O = Needs additional work

SUMMARY

All the tests in this chapter are designed to give the teacher as much information as possible concerning her children's maturity level in perceptual skills. The tests are divided into levels for convenience in administering and should be used and adapted in any way that seems appropriate for a particular group or individual. The individual profile sheet and the class record sheets are intended as aids in recording and organizing the information gained.

FOUR

Receptive and Generative Language Skills

The student's ability to use language is an important factor in determining his success in the school setting. Both his academic work and his skill in social interaction are profoundly affected by his ability to communicate and to comprehend language. The student is encouraged to utilize language as a tool in every aspect of his school experience.

If the student is verbally competent, language skills may develop with rapidity and depth at an early age. Language sophistication is an important part of the child's development during the preschool years. Children vary in the language experiences they encounter before they enter school. In some homes and many nursery schools, children are exposed to and participate in challenging and meaningful language activity with peers, siblings, and adults and through contact with books and magazines as well. Through such contacts children develop a sound background in communicative skills. Thus many at the age of five or six have the language background necessary for successful school experience.

Beginning reading depends heavily on the child's vocabulary knowledge and his ability to use language. The child has to know the words used in basic readers and other texts in order to read them. Just as an adult would have a difficult time reading a research article in biochemistry if that field was not familiar to him, so does the child have difficulty with unfamiliar words. The job of the child in learning to read is vastly complicated if the words he encounters are not already part of his listening or oral vocabulary.

For some children, however, the home environment provides a minimum of language experience. The cultural heritage of the child and the socioeconomic background of his family have much to do with the language skills he develops. Recent studies indicate that various subcultures use language differently with respect to children. In some it is assumed that the child is a participant in verbal interactions, and he may be the focus of a great deal of conversational activity. In other subcultures the orientation might not call for frequent verbal response and the child may be rarely attentive to or included in the conversational matrix.

As with any skill, proficiency is directly related to exposure and practice. Thus various discussion techniques may be necessary to expose some children to oral language and to give them practice in it before they will be ready to begin formal reading instruction.

ECHOIC LANGUAGE SKILLS TEST

Echoic ability—the ability to repeat or echo

what one hears—appears to be quite significant in helping to determine the degree to which the child can listen and attend to language. Tests in this area can help the teacher determine whether a child needs additional instruction in oral language retention.

In the two echoic tests described below, it will be possible to get a clear picture of the importance of meaningful talk to the child by first measuring his ability to retain "talk" sounds without context clues (without sentences) and then with context rules.

The particular kind of memory task associated with the retention of languagelike nonsense sounds may be related to the child's ability to remember language that is meaningful to others but is novel to him. As adults we often forget that much of what the young child hears amounts to nonsense sounds for him; it is rather like listening to a conversation in an unusual foreign language. Nonsense echoic tests give us an insight into the child's ability to retain the language sounds he hears. Of course the first time he encounters a new word he may have difficulty in retaining the meaning, pronunciation, and nuances associated with its use. But, his retention of at least some aspects of the language will assist in the development of receptive vocabulary, both oral and written. We maintain that this in turn will help in the development of reading skills. The test of listening and repeating, then, is designed to measure a child's ability to retain the sound patterns of the words he hears without context clues.

Example: nonsense echoics
"Repeat after me." (Teacher reads entire item to child.)
1. Gerbal tee mars el cobb less mendel hoi.
2. Bendo, gasset ba male ur lebol deption.
Note: The child's responses can be recorded on the answer sheet according to this marking system: mispronunciation ~~cat~~; omission ~~cat~~; insertion cat; hesitation cat.

Echoics in meaningful language adds the context and organization of language patterns to the concept of sound units.

It is reasonable to expect a child to retain a much larger part of his meaningful listening environment than strings of sounds or words that are unrelated to meaning. As the child listens to more and more difficult material in this test, however, he mixes the words he does know with sounds that are fairly meaningless, though not nonsense words from his point of view. Therefore this test, perhaps more than any other, closely resembles what the child actually experiences in the process of acquiring language.

Example: meaningful language echoics
1. The arc light is most luminous.
2. The anesthetist utilized ether.
3. Tangential pro arguments rarely sway umpires.
4. Ubiquitous abbleskiuvers are eaten for breakfast.
5. Indefatigable gendarmes populate the ancient garrison.

TESTS OF LISTENING AND REPEATING (ECHOICS)

Note: Teacher marks each child's response according to the following directions:

omissions   two lines through word
mispronunciations   one line through word
insertions ∧ write in word
hesitations ~~~~ under word

Directions to the teacher:

This test must be given individually. Oral practice of the sentences will prove most helpful. A printed copy for use by the teacher will be necessary for each child in marking errors.

NOVEL (NONSENSE) CONTENT

Directions to the child:

Listen carefully. I will say some words. You may not understand the words, but say them back to me just the way I say them to you. (Repeat once if necessary.)

1. Dee pa set moss.
2. Tom foo líster sood.
3. Sima log num tee moster.
4. Bummer de prémig fílible.
5. Arpig, rítmoss con welloby.
6. Mimig pa zelder fummoxible.
7. Bolloby ut quillig vonimous.
8. Gerbal tee nars, el tobb les mendel-hoy.
9. Bindo, gasset ob róssitter.
10. Régim unshillings, ur lebol déption.

TESTS OF LISTENING AND REPEATING (ECHOICS) FAMILIAR CONTENT

Directions to the child:

Listen carefully. I will say each sentence twice. Then you say it back to me. Try to remember the words just as I say them. Then say them back to me just as I do.

1. Bear cubs climb trees.
2. Careful work pays big dividends.
3. Seldom does the crow fly over the hawk.
4. Let's hie ourselves to the market place.
5. In the last analysis, your observations were correct.
6. It is selfish of you to think only of your own hunger.
7. With little evasive action, the robber quit the scene of the crime.
8. What is the most explicit direction you have ever received for that task?
9. Robert and a company of ruffians advanced up the dimly lit causeway.
10. In the conclusion, the story gives little comfort to the bewildered reader.
11. With long strides the boys covered the frozen ground in good time, leaving little trace of their passage.
12. The arc light casts eerie shadows over the rough–hewn edifice.
13. The anesthetist utilized ether in the long and sensitive appendectomy.
14. Tangential pro arguments rarely sway umpires.
15. Indefatigable gendarmes populate the ancient garrison.

GENERATIVE LANGUAGE SKILLS TEST

A child's ability to generate language that is appropriate to a given situation is quite central to the skills utilized in reading. Measures of generative language skills include: (1) the number of words used, (2) the sentence structures associated with the words used, and (3) the appropriateness of the words and structures.

It is frequently found that the larger the number of words and expression patterns available to the child in oral speaking, the larger his reading vocabulary. A variety of expressions contributes not only to accuracy in the child's use of oral language but to his ability to comprehend written language as it grows more sophisticated. The child's flexibility with language can be measured, for example, by the number of synonyms utilized in the description of particular stimulus pictures.

Three subtests of generative language skill are suggested: (1) variety of language, (2) quantity of language, and (3) accuracy of oral language usage.

In the Variety of Oral Language Test, the child is given increasingly complex drawings and is asked to describe them. When the child utilizes certain words in his descriptions, the teacher checks them on the tally sheet.

In the Quantity of Oral Language Test, the child is given another set of pictures and is asked to tell what is happening. In this instance, the number of words used by the child is the teacher's criterion.

In the Accuracy of Oral Language Test, the child is asked to use as many words as he can that tell about a particular object or scene pictured. As he uses certain key words, his score increases. An appropriate score sheet is provided.

An example of each type of test is included. Other pictures can be chosen by the teacher as she desires.

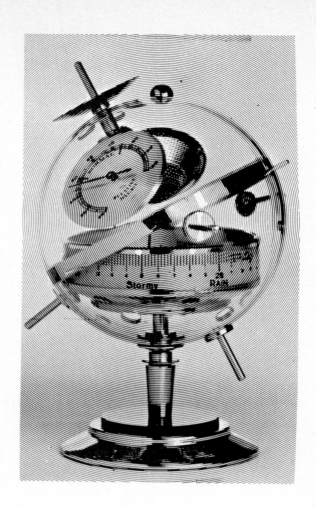

GENERATIVE LANGUAGE SKILLS TEST

Part 1   VARIETY OF ORAL LANGUAGE (INDIVIDUAL) (see page 207)

Note: A relatively complex picture such as the one on this sheet will be used with children in intermediate and upper grades. A simpler picture should be used with primary grade children.

Directions to the teacher:

Show the picture to the child. As he describes the picture, note the number of different words he uses by scoring them on the tally sheet.

Directions to the child:

What do you see here?

Part 2   GENERATIVE LANGUAGE SKILLS

———————— axis

———————— ball

———————— clock

———————— dial

———————— glass

———————— hand

———————— handle

———————— rod

———————— screw

———————— socket

———————— sphere

———————— station

———————— tube

———————— vane

———————— weather

GENERATIVE LANGUAGE SKILLS

Part 2   QUANTITY OF ORAL LANGUAGE (INDIVIDUAL) (see page 208)

Directions to the teacher:

Show the child a picture that depicts action, such as the one below. Record the total number of words, including repetitions, the child uses to describe it.

Directions to the child:

What is happening here? (When he stops talking, the teacher waits ten seconds and says: Is there anything else you can say about what is happening here?

TALLY SHEET

Part 2 GENERATIVE LANGUAGE SKILLS

_____   _____   _____   _____   _____
_____   _____   _____   _____   _____
_____   _____   _____   _____   _____
_____   _____   _____   _____   _____
_____   _____   _____   _____   _____
_____   _____   _____   _____   _____
_____   _____   _____   _____   _____
_____   _____   _____   _____   _____
_____   _____   _____   _____   _____
_____   _____   _____   _____   _____
_____   _____   _____   _____   _____
_____   _____   _____   _____   _____

Part 3 ACCURACY OF ORAL LANGUAGE (INDIVIDUAL)

Directions to the teacher:

Show the child a picture.

Directions to the child:

Tell me what you see in this picture. Tell me all about the thing I point to. (The teacher points to each thing until the child stops talking about it.)

GENERATIVE LANGUAGE TEST

Part 3 ACCURACY OF ORAL LANGUAGE *(see pages 209-210)*

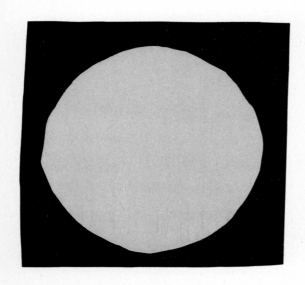

GENERATIVE LANGUAGE TEST

Part 3   ACCURACY OF ORAL LANGUAGE (see page 211)

Tally Sheet

PICTURE #1	PICTURE #2	PICTURE #3
_____ circle	_____ parallel	_____ angle
_____ round	_____ parallelogram	_____ line
_____ line	_____ line	_____ straight
_____ closed	_____ straight	_____ blue
_____ plane	_____ side	_____ red
_____ center	_____ angle	_____ white
_____ equidistant	_____ four	_____ purple
_____ arc	_____ acute	_____ round
_____ yellow	_____ obtuse	_____ curved
_____ blue	_____ equal	_____ birds
	_____ equilateral	_____ mountains
	_____ plane	_____ sun
	_____ red	_____ rising
	_____ green	_____ light
	_____ orange	_____ stream
	_____ wavy	
	_____ pointed	
	_____ scalloped	

TEST ON FOLLOWING DIRECTIONS

Much of everyone's life activities involve a great deal of listening. Especially in the school, a majority of learning takes place through listening. It has been estimated that 65 percent of all classroom time involves a teacher lecturing, in which the child's acquisition of information and concepts are naturally by means of a listening process. As teachers we often give directions, explain concepts, and correct homework orally. We expect the children to understand and follow through on what we have said. But many times have we been interrupted by that familiar, "Teacher, what do I do now?" Not listening? While that is often the case there is also the possibility that we gave too many directions for that child, spoke too fast, or used words or concepts that the child did not understand.

Because we do depend on the child's listening skills so much of the time, it makes sense to have some idea of what he can understand and follow orally. In addition, the process of following written directions must begin with the appropriate application of oral ones. A test to ascertain the child's ability to follow oral directions can save the teacher time and temper.

Children are provided in this test with a simple set of materials and are asked to perform tasks related to those materials after directions are given. The ability to follow short and long directions to perform specific actions is tested.

The first directions are as simple as "Hold up the yellow one." Later, the number and complexity of directions increase to include both lengthy sequences of words and words whose meanings may be inferred from the context but may not be specifically known by the listener.

TEST ON FOLLOWING DIRECTIONS

Directions to the teacher:

This test can be administered individually or in small groups. A child scores one point for each item he completes correctly in all parts. A tally sheet is one easy way to note each child's score. Analysis of the results is especially profitable in this test both for the number of directions that a child can follow and for key words which he has difficulty following, such as first, second, half, over, under, and so on. Each child will need a pencil, three sheets of paper, five crayons—red, green, blue, yellow, and black—and a book. A sample tally sheet follows.

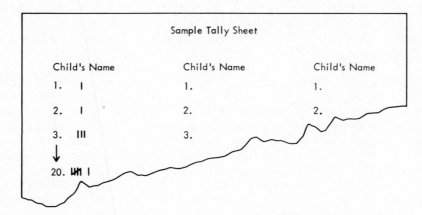

Sample Tally Sheet

Child's Name	Child's Name	Child's Name
1. I	1.	1.
2. I	2.	2.
3. III	3.	
↓		
20. ⊬Ħ I		

Directions to the children:

Today we're going to see how well you can listen and follow directions. Be sure you have these things on your desk. (Hold up each item and name it as children check.) Now I am going to give you some directions. Listen carefully, and when I finish and say "begin" do exactly what I said. Do not start until I say "begin."

Note: The words in bold type indicate the direction being given. The number in parentheses indicates how many directions are present in this item.

(1)   1. **Hold up** your pencil. Begin.

(2)   2. **Put** your pencil **on** your desk. Begin.

(3)   3. **Open** the book and **put** in the paper. Then **close** the book. Begin.

(4)   4. **Take** the paper out of the book, **fold** it in **half** and **make** a black dot on it. Begin.

(4)   5. Take your **red crayon** and **make a square over** the black dot. **Color** the square green. Begin.

(5)	6.	**Make three triangles** with your **blue crayon.** Color the first triangle **red** and the **second triangle green.** Begin.
(5)	7.	**Copy every other letter** from the **title** of your book **on the top** of your paper with a **pencil.** Begin.
(6)	8.	Take your **second sheet** of paper and **fold** it in **half. Unfold** it and **draw a line** with your **yellow crayon on the crease.** Begin.
(6)	9.	At the **top of** your paper make a **green circle** with a **red X** in the **center. Make a blue square under** the circle. Begin.
(6)	10.	**Print your name with pencil** at the **bottom** of your paper. Now **cross out** the **third letter** with a **black crayon.** Begin.
(7)	11.	**Put** your book **face down on the desk** and **trace** the edge of the book **on your** paper **with a pencil. Draw lines diagonally** across the paper **from the corners.** Begin.
(7)	12.	**Count** the windows on the **(choose direction)** side of the wall and make a **green square** to represent each window. **Color** each square a **different** color but make the **last square black.** Begin.
(8)	13.	**Put your papers** in the **top right hand corner** of your desk. **Put** the book **on top** of the papers. Put your pencil **next to** your book and **put** the crayons **under** the book. Begin.
(8)	14.	**Open** the book to **page 8. Write** the **second** word on the **first line** in **blue** on the paper and **fold** it in **half.** Begin.
(11)	15.	**Make four** lines each of a **different** color on **one side** of your **third** paper. Then **turn it** over and **print your** name in **pencil** on the other side. **Fold** it in **half** and **put it** in the book, **back of page** 20. Begin.

LISTENING COMPREHENSION TESTS

Following directions is very important in the school setting, but other types of listening comprehension have as much or more impact on the child's learning level. The acquisition of reading skills and language pertinent to his life comes to a large extent from the child's need to assimilate what he hears and then to recall the situation under which it was heard in order to understand and use the information. Tests help the teacher determine the level at which the child understands.

Oral language can be useful both in determining the child's potential level of reading comprehension and in discovering gaps in his comprehension skills that may be reflected in reading tasks.

Many times it is not possible to tell how much a child understands through a regular silent reading test. After all, if the words get in the way his opportunity for understanding is greatly decreased. For example, if a child gets a low score on a social studies test, it is difficult to determine if the problem was the child's understanding of the subject matter or his inability to read the material offered.

In giving a listening comprehension test we ask the question, "If he could read this material, would he actually be able to understand it?" If he cannot understand while listening, there is little reason to believe that he will be able to do so when he is reading similar material. In the same way, we may find particular skills the child lacks and thus be able to pinpoint problem areas in comprehension apart from the additional complications of the reading process itself.

The Listening Comprehension Test is divided into three parts: (1) the recall of general information, (2) the interpretation of oral language, and (3) the inferential analysis of oral language.

The first part of the test is divided into the recall of sequence and the recall of setting and character. The recall of sequence has to do with the proper order of events in a series of words or in a meaningful sentence or paragraph that is read to the child. The scoring criterion is the correspondence of the ideas. In this test the child's answer sheet has pictures of various objects named in the series or sentences. His job is to number the pictures in the correct sequence so that if the story is reread the sequence would follow the story. The second subtest seeks to determine the child's ability to recall the nature of the people and animals in the story and the other features of the setting that are of particular importance in determining the author's purpose. The statements are arranged in increasing complexity. The listener's ability to determine with accuracy the words that best describe the characters portrayed and to recall the words actually used by the author will be the scoring criteria.

The next test is developed to assess the ability to interpret the material at hand. The insightful understanding of the meaning behind stated information is an asset closely related to the understanding and use of both oral and written language. Alternative interpretations are presented after each paragraph in this section, and the child is asked to choose one. His ability to use synonyms for words and to use phrases that summarize, generalize, and categorize the words and ideas presented constitute interpretive listening comprehension.

The last test in the listening series asks the child to draw inferences from statements and to judge what are the most likely ways to conclude incomplete statements. His ability to make judgments and to determine the author's "next step" is the subject of the examination. High, medium, and low scores should be determined by the teacher with regard to her own curriculum goals.

LISTENING COMPREHENSION TEST

Directions to the teacher:

The various parts of this test may be given to individuals or groups. Children will have an answer sheet to mark. Since this is a listening test, however, the answers must be read to the children as well as the original material (except for section A of part 1, where picture clues are used). It is sometimes necessary to practice reading the material in advance to avoid mispronunciations and to avoid stressing a particular answer. You may repeat once.

Part 1   Direct Recall of Information

Section A   Recall of Sequence

Directions to the children:

Today you are going to have to be good listeners and remember what I read to you. After I read, I will ask you to put some numbers in front of pictures that tell the order in which you heard the words I said. Don't do any writing until I say "begin." Let's try sample A. Listen to the words I say: "dog, bird, cloud." Now, put a one in front of the picture of the first word I said, and a two in front of the second word. (Pause.) Listen again: dog, bird, cloud. Did you put a one in front of the picture of the dog? What did you put the two in front of? What would you put in front of the picture of the cloud? Good! (Check answers to make sure they all understand.) Let's begin now.

Part 1   Section A   WORD LIST   RECALL OF SEQUENCE

Sample A —   dog, bird, cloud.
1.   —   car, house.
2.   —   boy, rabbit, dog.
3.   —   The wall is by the fence.

4.   —   The girl and the cat sat in front of the tree.

5.   —   The horse and the dog ran over the hill to the house.

6.   —   The fountain by the house has birds and butterflies on it.

7.   —   The many–colored leaves are falling from the trees and the children are raking them.

8.   —   Put your comb and brush on the table and sit in the chair by the fireplace.

9.   —   The train passed two houses, a barn, and a tree as it sped along.

10.   —   The book is about a rabbit, a dog, and a boy who lived in the forest by the hills.

LISTENING COMPREHENSION TEST *(see page 212)*

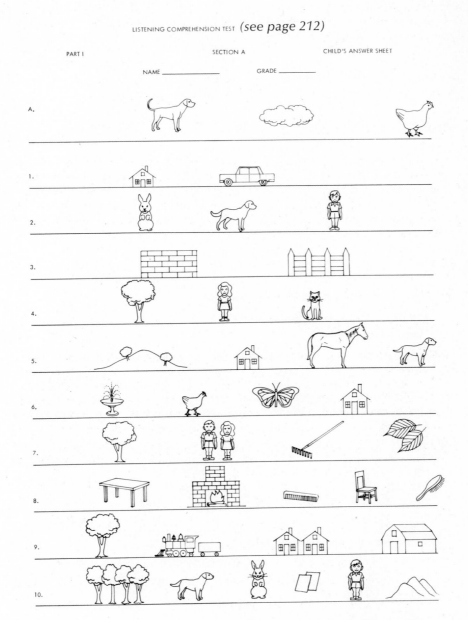

PART I   SECTION A   CHILD'S ANSWER SHEET

NAME _____   GRADE _____

LISTENING COMPREHENSION TEST

Part 1   DIRECT RECALL OF INFORMATION

Section B   Recall of Setting and Character

Directions to the teacher:

The story material, the questions, and the possible answers must be read to the children. Even if a child can read them himself, he should hear the material. You may repeat once. Each child will need a copy of the test.

Directions to the children:

Listen carefully. When I'm through I will read the questions and answers and you will circle the answer to each question. Don't circle anything until I read the questions and answers. Let's try the sample. Listen: "The white cat caught the little gray mouse." On your answer sheet, question A states, "The cat was (1) little, (2) white, (3) gray." Circle one of the answers. Question B says, "The mouse was (1) white, (2) tiny, (3) gray." Circle one of the answers. Which was the correct answer about the cat? (Let the children answer.) Which was the correct answer about the mouse? Good! Now we'll do the rest.

Part 1   Section B

STORIES AND QUESTIONS

Sample: The white cat caught the little gray mouse.

    A.   The cat was (1) little (2) white (3) gray.
    B.   The mouse was (1) white (2) tiny (3) gray.

Read:

The sleepy dog sat watching the old cowhand.
1.   The dog was: (1) old (2) gray (3) sleepy (4) soft.
2.   The cowhand was: (1) young (2) sleepy (3) tall (4) old.

The soft gray light of morning woke me from my dreams.
3.   The person talking was: (1) eating (2) dreaming (3) yawning (4) hopping.
4.   The time of day is: (1) morning (2) afternoon (3) night (4) summer.
5.   The morning light is: (1) gray (2) white (3) hard (4) soft. (Note two possible answers.)

The tall man walked quickly up the brick stairs and into the dusty old house.
6.   The house was: (1) new (2) dirty (3) old (4) fancy.
7.   The man was: (1) young (2) tall (3) fast (4) jumpy.
8.   The stairs were: (1) steep (2) dusty (3) brick (4) stone.

The two children ran and jumped in the leaves, laughing happily. Their dogs chased their tails till they were exhausted.
9.   The children were: (1) quick (2) exhausted (3) happy (4) sitting.
10.   The dogs were: (1) running (2) chasing (3) jumping (4) exhausted. (Note two possible answers.)

11.   The ground was covered with: (1) grass ② leaves (3) flowers (4) dogs.

In those last solemn moments before they parted, the two men sat staring intensely at the half–empty glasses on the table in the now silent room.

12.   The room was: (1) silent (2) lonely (3) intense ④ silent.
13.   The men were: (1) talking ② staring (3) sitting (4) drinking.
14.   The glasses were: (1) half full ② half empty (3) completely full (4) completely empty.
15.   The men are going to: (1) sing (2) drink ③ part (4) join.

LISTENING COMPREHENSION TEST (see page 213)

Part 1   Section B

CHILD'S ANSWER SHEET

Name _____   Grade _____

Sample

      A.   The cat was: (1) little (2) white (3) gray.
      B.   The mouse was (1) white (2) tiny (3) gray.

---

1.   The dog was: (1) old (2) gray (3) sleepy (4) soft.
2.   The cowhand was: (1) young (2) sleepy (3) tall (4) old.

3.   The person talking was: (1) eating (2) dreaming (3) yawning (4) hopping.
4.   The time of day is: (1) morning (2) afternoon (3) night (4) summer.
5.   The morning light is: (1) gray (2) white (3) hard (4) soft.

6.   The house was: (1) new (2) dirty (3) old (4) fancy.
7.   The man was: (1) young (2) tall (3) fast (4) jumpy.
8.   The stairs were: (1) steep (2) dusty (3) brick (4) stone.

9.   The children were: (1) quick (2) exhausted (3) happy (4) sitting.
10.   The dogs were: (1) running (2) chasing (3) jumping (4) exhausted.
11.   The ground was covered with: (1) grass (2) leaves (3) flowers (4) dogs.

12.   The room was: (1) deserted (2) lonely (3) intense (4) silent.
13.   The men were: (1) talking (2) staring (3) sitting (4) drinking.
14.   The glasses were: (1) half full (2) half empty (3) completely full (4) completely empty.
15.   The men are going to: (1) sing (2) drink (3) part (4) join.

Part 2   INTERPRETATION OF ORAL LANGUAGE

Directions to the teacher:

The test may be given to individuals or groups. Read the story material, questions, and answers to the children. The material may be repeated once. Each child needs an answer sheet.

Directions to the children:

I'm going to read you some sentences. After I read them to you I will read the questions and the answers that are on your page. When I finish you will circle the answers that are correct. Let's try the sample. Listen. "Joe was mean, heartless, and less than a friend to the children." (Read the sentence twice.) The question on your page is: "Sample A. How would you describe Joe? (1) lazy, (2) careful, (3) old, (4) cruel." Circle the correct answer. (Repeat once if necessary.) All right. What was the correct answer? Good! Now we'll do the rest.

Stories and Questions

The horses were sweating heavily as they strained and tugged at the heavy load.

1. The horses were: (1) resting (2) playing (3) working.
2. They felt: (1) cross (2) hot (3) tired.

The man shouted at the children who hurriedly ran away, trembling and shaking.

3. The children were: (1) noisy (2) frightened (3) angry (4) happy.
4. The man was: (1) angry (2) calm (3) hurried (4) gentle.

The soft light of dawn caused the rooster to crow noisily, waking the cowhand rudely.

5. The time was: (1) evening (2) summer (3) morning (4) afternoon.
6. The cowhand had been: (1) working (2) sleeping (3) eating (4) rude.

The young girl sighed deeply and a tear rolled down her cheek as she looked at the picture of the handsome young man in his gray uniform.

7. The girl is: (1) sick (2) happy (3) sad (4) crazy.
8. The girl is probably: (1) lonely (2) busy (3) an actress (4) his mother.
9. The young man is probably: (1) a soldier (2) a photographer (3) her father (4) with the girl.

"The book is too difficult for me," said Jane. "I will go to Jim and have him explain it to me."

10. Jane thinks: (1) Jim can read (2) Jim is tall (3) Jim is kind (4) Jim is busy.
11. Jane wants Jim to: (1) read to her (2) help her understand (3) return her book (4) go to the library.

Back and forth, back and forth swayed the mast of the ship as the waves beat the hull and tore at the decks. "Lower away!" called the captain as the lashing continued.

12. The ship is: (1) old and cracked (2) in a storm (3) on a cruise (4) falling apart.
13. The captain is: (1) abandoning the ship (2) radioing for help (3) putting the sailors to work (4) going to sleep.

With coats gleaming in the bright sun, the mare and her colt raced across the green pasture seemingly for the sheer pleasure of being alive, while deep in the forest thousands of newly hatched insects scurried from beneath the damp moss-covered logs.

14. The main message of this story is: (1) the coming of winter (2) how bugs are different from horses (3) how colorful the day was (4) the power and contrast in young life.
15. Young animals live: (1) only in pasture and under logs (2) in large numbers (3) only if they can run fast (4) in many different conditions.

LISTENING COMPREHENSION TEST (see page 214)

Part 2   CHILD'S ANSWER SHEET

Name _____   Grade _____

Sample A

How would you describe Joe?

(1) lazy (2) careful (3) old (4) cruel

1. The horses were: (1) resting (2) playing (3) working.
2. They felt: (1) cross (2) hot (3) tired.

3. The children were: (1) noisy (2) frightened (3) angry (4) happy.
4. The man was: (1) angry (2) calm (3) hurried (4) gentle.

5. The time was: (1) evening (2) summer (3) morning (4) afternoon.
6. The cowhand had been: (1) working (2) sleeping (3) eating (4) rude.

7. The girl is: (1) sick (2) happy (3) sad (4) crazy.
8. The girl is probably: (1) lonely (2) busy (3) an actress (4) his mother.
9. The young man is probably: (1) a soldier (2) a photographer (3) her father (4) with the girl.

10. Jane thinks: (1) Jim can read (2) Jim is tall (3) Jim is kind (4) Jim is busy.
11. Jane wants Jim to: (1) read to her (2) help her understand (3) return her book (4) go to the library.
12. The ship is: (1) old and cracked (2) in a storm (3) on a cruise (4) falling apart.
13. The captain is: (1) abandoning the ship (2) radioing for help (3) putting the sailors to work (4) going to sleep.

14. The main message of this story is: (1) the coming of winter (2) how bugs are different from horses (3) how colorful the day was (4) the power and contrast in young life.
15. Young animals live: (1) only in pasture and under logs (2) in large numbers (3) only if they can run fast (4) in many different conditions.

Part 3   INFERENTIAL ANALYSIS OF ORAL LANGUAGE

Directions to the teacher:

Read the story material and questions and answers to the children. Each child should have an answer sheet but should not read and answer questions independently. Material may be reread as necessary. Check the answers after number 1 to make sure all the children understand the directions.

Directions to the children:

I am going to read some sentences to you, each of which has a special meaning. Then I will read some questions and answers about the sentences. Do not mark your paper until after I have read the answers. Then put an X on the line in front of the most correct answer. Listen carefully.

1. "A penny saved is a penny earned."

   What does that sentence mean?

   _____ If you save money you will only get pennies.
   _____ If you save money you can be a coin collector.
   ___X___ If you save money it is as if you had earned it.

2. "If you are careful, the life you save may be your own."

   What should the reader do, according to that statement?

   _____ Live a long time.
   _____ Be careful and save the lives of others.
   ___X___ Realize that if he is careless he will endanger his life as well as other people's lives.

3. "A stitch in time saves nine."

   The statement means:

   _____ You should learn to sew.
   ___X___ Fixing something right away will keep it from getting worse.
   _____ In time things will get better.

4. "Time heals all wounds."

   This probably means:

   _____ Your cuts and bruises will get better.
   _____ We need to learn first aid.
   ___X___ We will forget about the things that have hurt us after awhile.

5. "The early bird gets the worms."

   This tells us:

   ___X___ If we do something right away it will work out better for us.
   _____ Birds get up early.
   _____ Worms are good to eat.

6. The lumberjack stepped back from the tree as it started to fall and _____ _____.

   What is likely to happen next?

   _____ ran away.
   _____ hit the tree again.
   _____ sharpened his ax.
   ___X___ yelled "timber."

7. The rain had been falling for hours when a cold north wind started to blow. The rain _____.

   What is likely to happen next?

   _____ stopped.
   ___X___ turned to ice.
   _____ melted.
   _____ caused a flood.

8. Johnny walked through the thick brush to get to his house.

   Days later he discovered that:

   ___X___ he had poison oak.
   _____ he had a snake bite.
   _____ he was lost.
   _____ he was hungry.

9. The children saw a jagged flash of lightning across the sky.

   They knew they would soon hear:

   _____ a horn.
   _____ yelling.
   ___X___ thunder.
   _____ a policeman.

10. The Brown family was out on the lake in their boat.

    All was quiet until Johnny yelled:

    ___X___ "I caught a fish."
    _____ "I'm sleepy."
    _____ "I want to go to school."
    _____ "I see a pretty cloud."

LISTENING COMPREHENSION TEST (see page 215)

Part 3   *CHILD'S ANSWER SHEET*

Name _____   Grade _____

1. What does that sentence mean?

   _____ If you save money you will only get pennies.
   _____ If you save money you can be a coin collector.
   _____ If you save money it is as if you had earned it.

2. What should the reader do, according to that statement?

   _____ Live a long time.
   _____ Be careful and save the lives of others.
   _____ Realize that if he is careless he will endanger his life as well as other people's lives.

3. The statement means:

   _____ You should learn to sew.
   _____ Fixing something right away will keep it from getting worse.
   _____ In time things will get better.

4. This probably means:

   _____ Your cuts and bruises will get better.
   _____ We need to learn first aid.
   _____ We will forget about the things that have hurt us after awhile.

5. This tells us:

   _____ If we do something right away it will work out better for us.
   _____ Birds get up early.
   _____ Worms are good to eat.

6. What is likely to happen next?

_____ ran away.
_____ hit the tree again.
_____ sharpened his ax.
_____ yelled "timber."

7. What is likely to happen next?

_____ stopped.
_____ turned to ice.
_____ melted.
_____ caused a flood.

8. Days later he discovered that:

_____ he had poison oak.
_____ he had a snake bite.
_____ he was lost.
_____ he was hungry.

9. They knew they would soon hear:

_____ a horn.
_____ yelling.
_____ thunder.
_____ a policeman.

10. All was quiet until Johnny yelled:

_____ "I caught a fish."
_____ "I'm sleepy."
_____ "I want to go to school."
_____ "I see a pretty cloud."

SUMMARY

Once a teacher has given these tests to a child, she should have a better idea of what listening comprehension skills the child already possesses that he can take with him to the printed page. If he has difficulties with these skills or in following directions, it is possible to plan work that will teach and reinforce the skills he needs, since such problems will be reflected and probably even heightened when the child attempts to utilize the same processes on the printed page.

H= High Proficiency
M= Medium Proficiency
L = Low Proficiency or
# of items correct

STUDENTS

	Nonsense Echoics	Familiar Echoics	Variety of Oral Lang.	Quantity of Oral Lang.	Accuracy of Oral Lang.	Following Directions	Recall of Sequence - A	Recall of Sequence - B	Interpretation of Oral Lang.	Inferential Analysis of Oral Lang.									

FIVE

Phonics and Word Analysis

A substantial body of research suggests that emphasis on the phonetic bases of English is a most productive way to teach beginning reading skills. Certainly it is true that most methods of teaching reading include some consideration of letter-sound relationships.

As we have seen, the child at the outset of his language experiences acquires a vocabulary and a grammatical style through oral communication. The meanings of words and the associations of these meanings with experience is acquired through listening and speaking. Only after a vocabulary and a style are firmly established can instruction in reading be fruitful. Therefore a first step in the development of reading skills must be the recall of oral language and its association with written language. As the child encounters the printed word, his past experience becomes a guide to the decoding process.

A second step in reading is the recognition of letter-sound relationships. English, like many languages, is based on phonetics; the letters in most instances correspond to the sounds of the words they spell. These letter-sound relationships are fundamental to the understanding of English in print.

Linguists have used the term "phoneme" to represent the individual sounds in language. The term "grapheme" is used to denote the written symbol associated with a particular speech sound. Phoneme-grapheme correspondence is quite orderly and pre-

dictable in most cases. The mastery and internalization of these relationships represents a significant step in the development of the child's reading skills.

The analysis of words is necessarily a part of a higher-order reading process. The child learns to identify the root word and to associate possible meanings with it. The analysis of affixes is also a vital part of the process of comprehension. Prefixes, suffixes, and inflectional endings contribute to the meaning of a word in very specific ways.

The ability of the child to pronounce a particular word is enhanced by his ability to understand word structure. If we think of the decoding process as a set of problem-solving strategies, we can see that the pairing of oral language with the meaningful interpretation of symbols requires a high level of skill. This process necessarily involves a relatively complex structure of thought that includes recognizing letters and words as such, translating those letters into sounds, recalling appropriate oral language patterns, and matching those language patterns to the sounds suggested by the print on the page.

Eventually these processes become automatic for the child, and his reading becomes smooth and fluent. But the beginning reader or the reader who needs remedial help often requires very specific training and practice in utilizing decoding skills.

Discovering which steps in the process

are causing a problem, however, poses for the teacher another kind of difficulty. Most programs teach decoding skills in a hierarchical order. An outline of these skills might appear as follows:

I. Sound-symbol relationships
   A. Consonant sounds
      1. Initial position: *b*at, *r*ug
      2. Ending position: ba*t*, ru*g*
   B. Blends and digraphs in similar positions
   C. Vowel sounds
      1. Short sounds in medial positions
      2. Long sounds in medial positions, and silent *e*
      3. Multiple spellings for vowel sounds
      4. Diphthongs
   D. Irregular spellings
II. Blending
   A. Single letters to words: *c-a-t*
   B. Blends to words: *sl-ee-t*
   C. Sound units: *n*ight, *l*ight
III. Syllabication
   A. Oral identification of number of parts in a word
   B. Rules for division of words
IV. Structural analysis
   A. Affixes
      1. Inflectional endings
         a. Plurals
         b. Verb endings: *ed, -ing, -s*
         c. comparisons: tall, tall*er*
      2. Prefixes: *un*happy
      3. Suffixes: announce*ment*
   B. Root words
      1. As an unchanged or little-changed part of longer words: *vary*, in*vari*ably

2. As a derivative from other languages: *tele-*: *tele*vision, *tele*phone, *tele*graph

Naturally the teacher may be working on several of these skills simultaneously. The beginning reader may, for example, be learning to recognize the letters and associate their sounds, and, at the same time, to blend single letters into words. He must start with the lower-level components within each skill, however, and if he misses a step in the process the development of his higher-level components is often impaired.

To discover the gaps, those missing steps, it is useful to have tests that will give us some specific information. The following groups of tests are designed to achieve that end.

ALPHABET RECOGNITION AND GENERATION TEST

The first part of this test requires the child to circle the letter the teacher names. The child is given a sheet with rows of letters. In many rows there are capital letters and lower-case letters. When the teacher says one of the letters the child merely circles it. Because no oral response is required this test can be administered to a group of children. In the second part of this test the child is asked to identify orally a particular letter in each row on the same paper—for example, "the last letter in row 2." Recall of the name of each letter is more difficult for the child than mere recognition. Because the response is oral this part must be given individually.

ALPHABET RECOGNITION TEST SPEECH TO PRINT

Directions to the teacher:

This test may be given to individuals or groups. Each child will need an answer sheet. Children may need a marker to stay in the correct row.

Directions to the children:

Listen to the names of the letters I say. Then find that letter and circle it. Let's try one. (1) Find number 1. (2) With your finger, point to all the letters I say. (3) Now find the letter A and circle it. Good! (Repeat, using the letters in the teacher pronunciation list.)

Teacher Guide Sheet
Pronunciation
List
_____

1.	A
2.	E
3.	T
4.	S
5.	L
6.	O
7.	V
8.	C
9.	F
10.	J
11.	W
12.	M
13.	G
14.	P
15.	B
16.	X
17.	D
18.	Q
19.	Y
20.	I
21.	N
22.	Z
23.	U
24.	R
25.	H
26.	K

Answer Sheet
_____

1.	A D C R B
2.	L M n E m
3.	l T f z r
4.	S G f z l
5.	V I T K F L
6.	c n o s p q
7.	X V r m N w
8.	c n i m e s
9.	K b h E L f
10.	i l J B N k
11.	m w p b z n
12.	n w t z m l
13.	a b D s G z d
14.	l P q n B g d
15.	D k q r p B g l
16.	w x z v y Y w K
17.	C r h u D c o n
18.	O d n m g R Q u
19.	Y v V W m N X i
20.	h T l t L b d n
21.	M n V w N e f j
22.	V n N u r q c z
23.	v U z g G w V x
24.	R G F m n D N z
25.	L r A E i H T X
26.	q L B F P V x K

ALPHABET RECOGNITION TEST

Part 1

Name _____   Grade _____

1.	A	D	C	R	B	
2.	L	M	n	E	m	
3.	l	T	f	z	r	
4.	S	G	f	z	l	
5.	V	I	T	K	F	L
6.	c	n	o	s	p	q
7.	X	V	r	m	N	w
8.	c	n	i	m	e	s
9.	K	b	h	E	L	F
10.	i	l	J	B	N	k
11.	m	w	p	b	z	n

58 *PHONICS AND WORD ANALYSIS*

12.	n	w	t	z	m	I		
13.	a	b	D	s	G	z	d	
14.	I	P	q	n	B	g	d	
15.	D	k	q	r	p	B	g	l
16.	w	x	z	v	y	Y	w	K
17.	C	r	h	u	D	c	o	n
18.	O	d	n	m	g	R	Q	u
19.	Y	v	V	W	m	N	X	i
20.	h	T	l	t	L	b	d	n
21.	M	n	V	w	N	e	f	j
22.	V	n	N	u	r	q	c	Z
23.	v	U	z	g	G	w	V	x
24.	R	G	F	m	n	D	N	z
25.	L	r	A	E	i	H	T	X
26.	q	L	B	F	P	V	x	K

ALPHABET GENERATION TEST
LETTER NAMES

Print to Speech

Note: An identical test can be constructed using lower-case rather than capital letters.

Directions to the teacher:

This test must be administered individually. Keep track of incorrect responses on a separate sheet.

Directions to the children:

Tell me the name of the letter that is underlined in each row.

1. A R
2. W T
3. F L f
4. W m N
5. P D B
6. r P Q O
7. Q S C G
8. I X L M
9. S T U V
10. V W A X
11. M A F B
12. p b c D
13. G t H d

14. d p q J
15. Y R n w
16. L M Z U
17. T S C P
18. V L X K
19. X A Y D
20. B D C E
21. N E H M
22. G C D U
23. R T P F
24. H E X L
25. V U W M
26. K Y E Z

Alphabet Check Sheet

√ = Child knows letter
O = Child does not know letter

STUDENTS	A	B	C	D	E	F	G	H	I	J	K	L	M	N	O	P	Q	R	S	T	U	V	W	X	Y	Z

60

LETTER-SOUND CORRESPONDENCE TESTS

The next tests involve letter-sound correspondence. The child begins them by identifying the initial consonant sounds in a list of words. Then single consonants at the end of a word are tested.

The next part involves the concept that when two or more consonants appear together they may produce a blended sound or a digraph. A blended sound can be thought of as two consonants slurred together that still retain most of their original sound value, as in *step*. A digraph, on the other hand, is a completely new sound produced by two consonants, as in *thin*. The original consonant sounds are completely lost.

Next a student's ability to recognize vowel sounds is tested. First come single vowel sounds that appear in the middle of a word in the consonant-vowel-consonant configuration.

The letter-sound correspondence tests described so far require that the child use a generative rather than a recognition response. They were designed for children with more advanced skills and require that the child write the letter or letters he thinks are the correct answers. A form of the letter-sound correspondence test for less advanced students is also included in this chapter. It does not require the writing of letters.

The Letter-Sound Generation Test is designed to test the child's ability to write the correct letter from a word clue. This test does not necessarily require a knowledge of spelling but rather an understanding of the letters related to particular sounds in words.

LETTER-SOUND CORRESPONDENCE TEST

Part 1   BEGINNING CONSONANTS

Directions to the teacher:

This test may be administered to groups or individuals. However, all items must be read to the children slowly, giving them ample opportunity to mark answers. Repeat as needed. Each child will need an answer sheet.

Directions to the children:

If the word I say begins with the sound of "b," put an X beside the number of the word on your answer sheet. Now listen. Number 1, "bat." Put an X in the box beside the 1 if you think bat begins with "b."

Sample A.   1. bat   2. cat   3. big   4. beautiful

Do you have an X beside number 1? Good! (Repeat for 2, 3, and 4.) You should not have an X beside number 2. Number 3 and number 4 should have an X in the boxes.

(Repeat for sample *B*, using the letter "t.")

Sample B.   5. dog   6. table   7. tunnel   8. mother

Letter Sounds

Beginning/Sound

r	9.	rattle	10.	rumble	11.	race	12.	where	13. table
t	14.	funny	15.	upset	16.	tumble	17.	laugh	18. fumble
p	19.	terrible	20.	parable	21.	tame	22.	careful	23. tall
f	24.	pancake	25.	flower	26.	done	27.	yell	28. flame
m	29.	flat	30.	elephant	31.	mouse	32.	near	33. mean
w	34.	water	35.	winter	36.	mind	37.	nobody	38. wear
s	39.	top	40.	sun	41.	sit	42.	caught	43. ear

d	44.	dog	45.	purple	47.	dapple	48.	dig	49.	zoo
h	50.	hill	51.	ring	52.	hot	53.	table	54.	marbles
j	55.	flip	56.	jump	57.	new	58.	jug	59.	Jill
l	60.	lamp	61.	log	62.	mother	63.	wind	64.	lady

LETTER-SOUND CORRESPONDENCE

Part 1   BEGINNING CONSONANTS

ANSWER SHEET

Name _____   Grade _____

Sample A

1. ☐   2. ☐   3. ☐   4. ☐

Sample B

5. ☐   6. ☐   7. ☐   8. ☐

9. ☐	10. ☐	11. ☐	12. ☐	13. ☐
14. ☐	15. ☐	16. ☐	17. ☐	18. ☐
19. ☐	20. ☐	21. ☐	22. ☐	23. ☐
24. ☐	25. ☐	26. ☐	27. ☐	28. ☐
29. ☐	30. ☐	31. ☐	32. ☐	33. ☐
34. ☐	35. ☐	36. ☐	37. ☐	38. ☐
39. ☐	40. ☐	41. ☐	42. ☐	43. ☐
44. ☐	45. ☐	47. ☐	48. ☐	49. ☐
50. ☐	51. ☐	52. ☐	53. ☐	54. ☐
55. ☐	56. ☐	57. ☐	58. ☐	59. ☐
60. ☐	61. ☐	62. ☐	63. ☐	64. ☐

Part 2   ENDING CONSONANTS

Directions to the children:

If the word I say ends with the sound of "t," put an X in the box beside the number of the word. Now listen. Number 1, "get." Put an X beside the 1 if you think "get" ends with the sound of "t." Do you have an X beside number 1? Good! (Repeat for 2, 3, and 4.)

Sample A   1. get   2. come   3. fat   4. forget

(Repeat directions above, using ending "r.")

Sample B   5. fun   6. bigger   7. gum   8. roam

Ending/Sound
s	9. light	10. useless	11. sold	12. cats
d	13. crossed	14. dune	15. rib	16. had
k	17. crank	18. kin	19. back	20. kite

n	21.	sharpen	22.	nail	23.	tan	24.	now
w	25.	whine	26.	nuisance	27.	willow	28.	slow
y	29.	quickly	30.	yellow	31.	you	32.	excite
p	33.	puppy	34.	pop	35.	group	36.	pan

LETTER-SOUND CORRESPONDENCE

Part 2   ENDING CONSONANTS

ANSWER SHEET

Name _____   Grade _____

Sample A

1. ☐   2. ☐   3. ☐   4. ☐

Sample B

5. ☐   6. ☐   7. ☐   8. ☐

9. ☐   10. ☐   11. ☐   12. ☐
13. ☐   14. ☐   15. ☐   16. ☐
17. ☐   18. ☐   19. ☐   20. ☐
21. ☐   22. ☐   23. ☐   24. ☐
25. ☐   26. ☐   27. ☐   28. ☐
29. ☐   30. ☐   31. ☐   32. ☐
33. ☐   34. ☐   35. ☐   36. ☐

Part 3   BLENDS AND DIGRAPHS

Directions to the children:

If the word I say has a "c-h" sound in it, put an X in the box beside the number of the word. Now listen. Number 1, "catch." Put an X beside the 1 if you think catch has a "c-h" in it. Do you have a X beside number 1? Good! Where is the "ch" sound? (Repeat for 2, 3, and 4. Check to be sure children can complete sample items.)

Sample A

1. catch   2. break   3. change   4. table

Sample B

(Repeat directions above, using "s-t.")

5. stop   6. taller   7. star   8. unstable

(Continue, pronouncing individual letters of blends and digraphs rather than their sounds.)

✓ = Knows sound
0 = Does not know sound

STUDENTS	b	d	f	h	j	l	m	p	r	s	t	w	t	r	s	d	k	n	w	y	p

Blended/Sound

sh	(digraph)	9.	show	10.	slow	11.	diminish	12.	set
tr	(blend)	13.	tender	14.	try	15.	timing	16.	train
sl	(blend)	17.	slide	18.	unslung	19.	slippery	20.	shine
ph	(digraph)	21.	phone	22.	place	23.	telegraph	24.	enough
gl	(blend)	25.	bleak	26.	glance	27.	unglued	28.	gum
br	(blend)	29.	brown	30.	bun	31.	grub	32.	nonbreakable
pr	(blend)	33.	pump	34.	proud	35.	practice	36.	upper
cl	(blend)	37.	closet	38.	cash	39.	cloud	40.	cleaner
sw	(blend)	41.	nonsense	42.	swing	43.	nose	44.	sing
ch	(digraph)	45.	reach	46.	shallow	47.	chirp	48.	rich
st	(blend)	49.	rinse	50.	stop	51.	false	52.	instant

LETTER-SOUND CORRESPONDENCE

Part 3   BLENDS AND DIGRAPHS

ANSWER SHEET

Name _____   Grade _____

Sample A

1. [ ]   2. [ ]   3. [ ]   4. [ ]

Sample B

5. [ ]   6. [ ]   7. [ ]   8. [ ]

9. [ ]   10. [ ]   11. [ ]   12. [ ]
13. [ ]   14. [ ]   15. [ ]   16. [ ]
17. [ ]   18. [ ]   19. [ ]   20. [ ]
21. [ ]   22. [ ]   23. [ ]   24. [ ]
25. [ ]   26. [ ]   27. [ ]   28. [ ]
29. [ ]   30. [ ]   31. [ ]   32. [ ]
33. [ ]   34. [ ]   35. [ ]   36. [ ]
37. [ ]   38. [ ]   39. [ ]   40. [ ]
41. [ ]   42. [ ]   43. [ ]   44. [ ]
45. [ ]   46. [ ]   47. [ ]   48. [ ]
49. [ ]   50. [ ]   51. [ ]   52. [ ]

Part 4   VOWEL SOUNDS   LEVEL I

(Individual administration)

Directions to the teacher:

This test must be administered individually. Keep record of answers on a separate sheet of paper.

Directions to the children:

Tell me what the middle sound is in the word "can." (Child responds with oral "a" or teacher says, "is it a?") Good. Now you say it—a. Good! Now let's try another. What is the middle sound in "bin"? (If the child doesn't respond, say "i" as in "bit." Then say:) Now you try it. Good.

TEACHER SCORE SHEET   LEVEL I

Sample A	can	Child's Name _____
Sample B	bin	Test Date _____

1. set		6. cute
2. cut		7. pine
3. pin		8. mope
4. mop		9. gape
5. gap		10. fate

Part 4   VOWEL SOUNDS   LEVEL I

(Group administration)

Directions to the teacher:

This test may be administered to small groups. Say the words clearly, but do not artificially stress the middle vowel. Check all samples to make sure children understand the instructions.

Directions to the children:

Tell me which words have the same middle sound. Here are three words.

1. bet   2. mess   3. bill

Which ones had the same middle sound? That's right, "bet" and "mess." Now look at *sample A.*

Sample A

1. call   2. red

The words are "call" and "red." Which one has the same sound as "bet" and "mess"? Right, "red." Put an X in the box next to "red" because it has the same middle sound.

Let's try again. Which of the next three words has the same middle sound?

1. kind   2. gull   3. mice

Right—"kind" and "mice." Now look at *sample B* on your paper. The words are "milk" and "file." Which one has the same middle sound as "kind" and "mice"? Yes, "file." So put an X in front of the word "file" because it has the same middle sound as "kind" and "mice." Now let's do the rest.

Teacher's Material

Sample A

bet, mess, bill
        answer: 1. call   2. <u>red</u>   (*Answer is underlined.*)

Sample B

kind, gull, mice
        answer: 1. milk   2. <u>file</u>

1. bale   pack   safe
    answer: bull <u>make</u>

2. cup   run   seem
    answer: feel <u>tug</u>

3. mut   mule   yule
    answer: <u>cute</u> but

4. grind   fin   like
    answer: cinder <u>finder</u>

5. call   mop   cod
    answer: <u>hot</u> roll

6. sole   mind   tote
    answer: <u>hole</u> run

7. site   set   fresh
    answer: mint <u>mend</u>

8. gap   make   pearl
    answer: girl <u>map</u>

9. yes   bit   sit
    answer: help <u>mill</u>

10. feel   peek   nice
    answer: <u>seek</u> fine

LETTER SOUND CORRESPONDENCE

Part 4   VOWEL SOUNDS   LEVEL II

ANSWER SHEET

Name _____   Grade _____

Sample A

1. ☐   call   2. ☐   red

Sample B

1. ☐   milk   2. ☐   file

1.   1. ☐   bull   2. ☐   make
2.   1. ☐   feel   2. ☐   tug
3.   1. ☐   cute   2. ☐   but
4.   1. ☐   cinder   2. ☐   finder
5.   1. ☐   hot   2. ☐   roll
6.   1. ☐   hole   2. ☐   run
7.   1. ☐   mint   2. ☐   mend
8.   1. ☐   girl   2. ☐   map
9.   1. ☐   help   2. ☐   mill
10. 1. ☐   seek   2. ☐   fine

Blends, Digraphs, and Vowels Check Sheet

V = Knows sound
O = Does not know sound

STUDENTS	ch	st	sh	tr	sl	ph	gl	br	pr	cl	sw	a	e	i	o	u	a	e	i	o	u

Blends and Diagraphs

Vowels

Short   Long

68

Directions to the teacher:

This test can be given to individuals or groups. The child needs merely a piece of paper and a pencil. Say the words clearly, but do not emphasize sounds artificially.

Part 1   A   INITIAL CONSONANTS

Directions to the children:

Write the letter at the beginning of the word I say.

1.	dog	11.	run
2.	ham	12.	note
3.	lamb	13.	fat
4.	pound	14.	win
5.	band	15.	tall
6.	man	16.	gone
7.	quick	17.	yellow
8.	sat	18.	jump
9.	vine	19.	zoo
10.	kit		

LETTER-SOUND GENERATION TEST

Part 1   A   INITIAL CONSONANTS

ANSWER SHEET

Name ─────────────   Grade ─────────

Directions

Write the letter at the beginning of the word I say.

1.		10.	
2.		11.	
3.		12.	
4.		13.	
5.		14.	
6.		15.	
7.		16.	
8.		17.	
9.		18.	
		19.	

V = Knows sound
O = Does not know sound

STUDENTS	d	h	l	p	b	m	qu	s	v	k	r	n	f	w	t	g	y	j	z				

Part 1 B   INITIAL CONSONANTS

Directions to the children:

After each number, I will say three words. Two of them will start with the same letter. You figure out the letter and write it beside the number.

1.	r	rattle	rumble	where
2.	t	shirt	tumble	tag
3.	p	pop	bond	pond
4.	f	fine	flower	time
5.	m	mean	near	mouse
6.	w	wind	painter	water
7.	d	boat	dime	don't
8.	h	haul	hike	pile
9.	l	little	lost	tag

Part 1 B   INITIAL CONSONANTS

ANSWER SHEET

Name ———————   Grade ———————

Directions to the children:

After each number I will say three words. Two of them will start with the same letter. You figure out the letter and write it beside the number.

1.
2.
3.
4.
5.
6.
7.
8.
9.

Part 2 A   ENDING CONSONANTS

Directions to the children:

Write the letter at the end of the word I say.

1.	nick	6.	door	11.	new
2.	rig	7.	ham	12.	men
3.	pastel	8.	careless	13.	jazz
4.	drop	9.	set		
5.	barb	10.	end		

Part 2 A ENDING CONSONANTS

ANSWER SHEET

Name _____ *Grade* _____

Directions to the children:

Write the letter at the end of the word I say.

1.
2.
3.
4.
5.
6.
7.
8.
9.
10.
11.
12.
13.

Part 2 B ENDING CONSONANTS

Directions to the children:

After each number I will say three words. Two of them will end with the same letter. You figure out the letter and write it beside the number.

1.	s	less	sold	cats
2.	d	rib	aud	bad
3.	k	back	link	kin
4.	n	tan	nail	sharpen
5.	w	slow	willow	news
6.	y	yellow	quickly	sticky
7.	p	pound	pop	lip
8.	g	gone	rig	bog
9.	l	wall	lawn	bill
10.	b	barn	cab	bib
11.	r	road	deliver	roar
12.	m	mom	man	seem
13.	t	ran	construct	rat

Part 2 B ENDING CONSONANTS

ANSWER SHEET

Name _____ *Grade* _____

Directions to the children:

After each number I will say three words. Two of them will end with the same letter. You figure out the letter and write it beside the number.

1.
2.
3.
4.
5.
6.
7.
8.
9.
10.
11.
12.
13.

Part 3 A   CONSONANT BLENDS AND DIGRAPHS

Directions to the teacher:

It may be necessary to do one or two items with the children to make sure that they understand the concept of a blend.

Directions to the children:

Write the two letters that form a blend sound at the beginning of the words I say.

1.	blast	11.	crock
2.	brown	12.	price
3.	drop	13.	slice
4.	fly	14.	snail
5.	fragile	15.	glance
6.	grass	16.	spice
7.	plaster	17.	smart
8.	stare	18.	swarm
9.	trinket	19.	sky
10.	closet	20.	sharp

Part 3 A   CONSONANT BLENDS AND DIGRAPHS

ANSWER SHEET

Name ＿＿＿＿＿＿＿   Grade ＿＿＿＿＿＿＿

Directions to the children:

Write the two letters which form a blend sound at the beginning of the words I say.

1.	11.
2.	12.
3.	13.
4.	14.
5.	15.
6.	16.
7.	17.
8.	18.
9.	19.
10.	20.

Ending Consonant Check Sheet

V = Knows sound
O = Does not know sound

STUDENTS

	k	g	l	p	b	r	m	s	t	d	w	h	z	y			

74

Part 3 B   CONSONANT BLENDS AND DIGRAPHS

Directions to the children:

After each number I will say three words. Two of them will have the same beginning two letters. You figure out the two letters and write them beside the number.

1.	black	block	born
2.	bronze	bull	brass
3.	drag	drink	end
4.	fine	flake	flower
5.	frog	elf	fresh
6.	grow	gay	green
7.	plow	lack	plank
8.	sign	stamp	stall
9.	trim	trick	tall
10.	car	climb	click
11.	crack	crane	cake
12.	proud	prize	peace
13.	save	slump	slice
14.	snarl	side	snake
15.	glow	glass	give
16.	sun	spare	spoon
17.	sock	smash	smile
18.	swirl	swap	safe
19.	sour	skate	skin
20.	ship	shine	sore
21.	phone	mark	philosophy
22.	change	shawl	champion
23.	salt	shine	sharp

LETTER-SOUND GENERATION TEST

Part 3 B   CONSONANT BLENDS AND DIGRAPHS

ANSWER SHEET

Name ———————————   Grade ————————

1.	13.
2.	14.
3.	15.
4.	16.
5.	17.
6.	18.
7.	19.
8.	20.
9.	21.
10.	22.
11.	23.
12.	

Consonant Blend and Digraph Check Sheet

V = Knows sound
O = Does not know sound

STUDENTS	ch	sh	bl	br	dr	fl	fr	gr	pl	st	tr	cl	cr	pr	sl	sn	gl	sp	sm	sw	sk	sh	ph

Part 4 A   VOWELS

Directions to the children:

Underline the letter that is in the middle of the word I say.

TEACHER		STUDENTS' CHOICE		
1.	safe	1. i	a	u
2.	sleep	2. e	o	a
3.	dime	3. o	u	i
4.	cone	4. a	o	e
5.	fume	5. u	i	e
6.	fat	6. i	u	a
7.	bell	7. a	e	i
8.	kit	8. i	a	o
9.	cob	9. o	u	i
10.	cup	10. a	u	e

LETTER-SOUND GENERATION TEST

Part 4 A   VOWELS

ANSWER SHEET

Name _____   Grade _____

1.	i	a	u
2.	e	o	a
3.	o	u	i
4.	a	o	e
5.	u	i	e
6.	i	u	a
7.	a	e	i
8.	i	a	o
9.	o	u	i
10.	a	u	e

BLENDING TEST

Blending tests attempt to determine the child's ability to listen to certain sounds and combine them with other sounds to form a new word. Being able to recognize or produce sounds in isolation does not necessarily mean that the child can then use them together to form a word. In fact, this is often a difficult task, particularly for the older child who is having reading problems. The task is of critical importance, however, in the child's development of independent word attack skills. In this test the child is asked to pair the ending of one word with the beginning of another. For example, the teacher may say, "I'm thinking of a word that ends like 'stoop' but it begins like 'cat.' Say the word." (The answer is "coop.")

Vowel Check Sheet

V = Knows sound
O = Does not know sound

STUDENTS

	Short					Long				
	a	e	i	o	u	a	e	i	o	u

78

V = Knows sound
O = Does not Know sound

STUDENT'S SKILLS

Dates Tested –

Beginning Consonants:
b
d
f
g
h
j
K
l
m
n
p
qu
r
s
t
v
w
y
z

Ending Consonants:
b
d
g
K
l
m
n
p
r
s
t
w
z

79

Blends, Digraphs, and Vowels
Individual Check Sheet

Child's Name_____

V = Knows sound
O = Does not know sound

Dates Tested -

STUDENT'S SKILLS

Consonant Blends and Diagraphs:

bl
br
ch
cl
cr
dr
fl
fr
gl
gr
ph
pl
pr
sh
sk
sl
sm
sn
sp
st
sw
tr

Short vowels:

a
e
i
o
u

Long vowels:

a
e
i
o
u

Directions to the teacher:

This test must be given individually unless the children are fairly adept at writing and spelling. Say the words clearly but do not stress the syllables.

Directions to the children:

Tell me the word that:

Starts like	and ends like	answer
1. net	best	nest
2. flat	new	flew
3. warren	steamer	warmer
4. come	seeing	coming
5. landed	running	landing
6. crane	fried	cried
7. into	convent	invent
8. counter	seated	counted
9. automatic	immobile	automobile

SYLLABICATION TEST

The test for knowledge of syllabication contains four levels. The first level tests the child's understanding of the concept that words contain parts that can be recognized. The child is asked to circle the number that corresponds to the number of parts he hears in a given word.

One- and two-syllable words appear at the beginning of the list. For example, if the teacher says the word "tiger" the child would circle the number 2 to indicate that the word has two parts. Words with multiple syllables such as "magnificent" and "corresponding" appear at the end of this level. The child's task in each case is to identify the number of syllables he hears.

The second level in the syllabication test has to do with the marking or selection of a particular syllable. For instance, the child is asked to draw a line after the first syllable in the word "unable" or before the last syllable in "climbing." The child will not be able just to count in order to mark correctly but he must have at least a rudimentary understanding of beginning and ending syllables.

The third part of the syllabication test has to do with dividing both long and short words into syllables without oral clues from the teacher. The child must utilize signals generated by the word itself.

In the first three tests, all the words used are meaningful words; they are potentially part of the child's speaking and reading vocabulary. In part 4, the child is asked to divide nonsense words into syllables. At this point the child must abstract the rules for dividing words into syllables. These words are, by design, familiar in configuration but are unfamiliar because they are not real words. Correctness is determined by standard syllable rules. Examples are "unritable" (un/rit/a/ble) and "contriding" (con/tri/ding).

Syllable rules that are tested are:

1. The number of vowel sounds in each word indicates the number of syllables. For example, shook, cur/tain, prob/a/bly.
2. A word is usually divided between the two consonants when double consonants occur between two vowels. For example, but/ter, hur/ry, let/ter.
3. Two different consonants are also divided if they occur between two vowels. For example, for/ward, pic/nic, cor/ner.
4. A consonant before an "-le" ending usually goes with the ending to form a syllable. For example, ta/ble, lit/tle, ap/ple.
5. A word is usually divided before the consonant when a single consonant appears between two vowels. For example, ba/by, ti/ger, mo/tor.
6. A blend or digraph is treated as one letter.

SYLLABICATION TEST   LEVEL I

Directions to the teacher:

This test may be administered to groups. Each child will need an answer sheet. Say each word clearly, but do not stress the syllables.

Directions to the children:

Listen for the number of parts or syllables in this word: "ta-ble." Listen again and watch my fingers. (Hold up one finger as each syllable is pronounced.) "Table." Do you hear the two parts? Good! Now look at sample *A*. Circle the 2 beside sample *A* because there are two parts (syllables) in "ta-ble."

Look at sample *B:* el-e-phant. How many parts are there? Three? Good! Circle the 3 beside sample *B*.

Circle the number of parts in each word as I pronounce it.

1.	canoe (2)	7.	whale (1)
2.	difficult (3)	8.	automobile (4)
3.	name (1)	9.	untie (2)
4.	ended (2)	10.	measurement (3)
5.	remove (2)	11.	magnificent (4)
6.	sky (1)	12.	corresponding (4)

SYLLABICATION TEST   LEVEL I
ANSWER SHEET

Name _____   Grade _____

Sample A   1   2   3   4

Sample B   1   2   3   4

1.	1	2	3	4	7.	1	2	3	4
2.	1	2	3	4	8.	1	2	3	4
3.	1	2	3	4	9.	1	2	3	4
4.	1	2	3	4	10.	1	2	3	4
5.	1	2	3	4	11.	1	2	3	4
6.	1	2	3	4	12.	1	2	3	4

SYLLABICATION TEST   LEVEL II

Directions to the teacher:

This test may be group-administered. All of the words should be read to the children, since they are not expected to be able to read the words.

Directions to the children:

Draw a line between the parts (syllables) in the words listed below. I will do the first sample for you. (Write on the board the word "window.") Listen to the word. "win-dow." Do you hear the two parts? "win-dow." Now you draw a line between the two parts on your sheet next to sample *A*. Let's try another: "un-tie." Do it on your paper by sample *B*.

Now draw a line after the first part (syllable) in these words. Listen carefully as I pronounce each word.

1. un/able
2. dis/mount
3. re/move
4. con/fine
5. house/boat
6. car/penter
7. run/ning
8. de/velopment

Draw a line before the last part (syllable) in these words. Listen carefully as I pronounce each word.

9. climb/ing
10. seat/ed
11. cost/ly
12. pit/cher
13. usa/ble
14. re/turn
15. win/dow
16. cafeteri/a

SYLLABICATION TEST   LEVEL II
ANSWER SHEET

Name _____   Grade _____

Draw a line after the first part (syllable) in these words.

Sample A   window

Sample B   untie

1. unable
2. dismount
3. remove
4. confine
5. houseboat
6. carpenter
7. running
8. development

Draw a line before the last part (syllable) in these words.

9. climbing
10. seated
11. costly
12. pitcher
13. usable
14. return
15. window
16. cafeteria

SYLLABICATION TEST   LEVEL III

Directions to the teacher:

The teacher reads the directions aloud while the children read them silently.

Directions to the children:

Read each word below and divide it into syllables by drawing a line between each syllable. For example, "undelivered" must be divided into four syllables like this: un/de/liv/ered. Divide each word below in the same way.

1. de/vel/op
2. whole/some
3. speed/o/me/ter
4. round/ed
5. light/er
6. float/ing
7. un/shrink/a/ble
8. re/charged
9. in/no/cent
10. ret/ro/grade
11. in/ter/pret
12. un/sus/pect/ing

SYLLABICATION TEST   LEVEL III
ANSWER SHEET

Name _____   Grade _____

Directions:

Read each word below and divide it into syllables by drawing a line between each syllable. For example, undelivered must be divided into four syllables like this: un/de/liv/ered.
Divide each word below in the same way.

1. develop
2. wholesome
3. speedometer
4. rounded
5. lighter
6. floating

7. unshrinkable
8. recharged
9. innocent
10. retrograde
11. interpret
12. unsuspecting

SYLLABICATION TEST   LEVEL IV

Directions to the teacher:

The teacher reads directions aloud while the children read them silently.

Directions to the children:

Divide each of the words below into syllables. You will not know what the words mean, but if you pronounce them to yourself silently this will help you to divide them correctly.

1. un/rit/ting
2. con/tri/ding
3. ruf/fing
4. mis/bel/ing
5. re/ti/min/ish
6. fum/ten

7. no/be/trun
8. yen/ti/tion
9. guel/lup
10. kan/mike
11. roun/bar/ning

SYLLABICATION TEST   LEVEL IV
ANSWER SHEET

Name _____   Grade _____

Directions:

Divide each of the words below into syllables. You will not know what the words mean, but if you pronounce them to yourself silently this will help you to divide them correctly.

1. unritting
2. contriding
3. ruffing
4. misbeling
5. retiminish
6. fumten

7. nobetrun
8. yentition
9. guellup
10. kanmike
11. rounbarning

STRUCTURAL ANALYSIS OF WORDS

In this test we are attempting to discover the child's knowledge of both root words and affixes as an aid to pronunciation and analysis of meaning. The child must develop a working definition of the nature of a root word and be able to identify examples. This implies that the child has decoding and comprehension skills that support each other in the problem-solving process of pronouncing a particular word. Once the root has been identified and labeled, the child's next task is to determine the affixes that contribute to the word's meaning. Again, the recognition of the affixes constitutes a significant clue to the pronunciation of the word as well as its meaning. For example, *dis*-oriented can be distinguished from *re*-oriented on the basis of configuration, and the definitions of the two words change according to the meaning of the affix, not the root word.

The first level of this test deals with the child's ability to identify roots within words. The test has rows of four words each. Three words have a common root. The child must underline these roots. The fourth word looks as if the root could be the same, but the meaning and/or pronunciation identify it as being different from the others. The child must cross out the word that does not belong to the group. For example:

re<u>count</u>   <u>count</u>less   co~~u~~ntry   un<u>counted</u>

The next level of this test deals with inflectional endings—their identification and their contribution to changes in meanings. For example, the child is asked to circle the word that is a plural:

baby   babies   baby's   babied

The next level deals with simple prefixes and suffixes and their identification. For instance, the child is asked to circle the word with a prefix that means "not":

happiness   unhappy   happily   happening

In the fourth level, both prefixes and suffixes are added to the words, which are arranged in a scrambled fashion. The affixes must be identified. For example, the prefix *dis*- must be correctly identified in "disconnect" and determined to be not present in "district."

STRUCTURAL ANALYSIS TEST   LEVEL I

Directions to the teacher:

The teacher reads aloud while the children read silently.

Directions to the children:

Underline the root word in each of the following words if the root word is present. Put an X on the word that does not have the root in it. Look at the sample. Notice that recount, countless, and uncounted have the same root and that country does not.

Sample

<u>recount</u>   <u>countless</u>   cou~~X~~try   <u>uncounted</u>

Now work the problems below in the same way:

1. un<u>marked</u>   re~~X~~ark   <u>marking</u>   <u>markproof</u>
2. li~~X~~en   un<u>listed</u>   <u>listing</u>   re<u>listed</u>
3. <u>alone</u>   <u>loner</u>   <u>lonely</u>   aba~~X~~ne
4. <u>parental</u>   <u>parentless</u>   trans~~X~~arent   <u>parents</u>
5. re<u>fasten</u>   <u>fasten</u>   fas~~X~~est   un<u>fasten</u>

6. eating   he~~X~~ter   eats   uneaten
7. kindly   unkindly   kin~~X~~ling   kindness
8. famed   famous   famously   fa~~X~~ine
9. painful   painless   painstaking   pa~~X~~ter
10. reader   reread   re~~X~~dy   reading

STRUCTURAL ANALYSIS TEST   LEVEL I
ANSWER SHEET

Name _____   Grade _____

Directions:

Underline the root word in each of the following words if the root word is present. Put an X on the word that does not have the root in it. Look at the sample. Notice that recount, countless, and uncounted have the same root and that country does not.

Sample

recount   countless   cou~~X~~try   uncounted

Now work the problems below in the same way:
1. unmarked   remark   marking   markproof
2. listen   unlisted   listing   relisted
3. alone   loner   lonely   abalone
4. parental   parentless   transparent   parents
5. refasten   fasten   fastest   unfasten
6. eating   heater   eats   uneaten
7. kindly   unkindly   kindling   kindness
8. famed   famous   famously   famine
9. painful   painless   painstaking   painter
10. reader   reread   ready   reading

STRUCTURAL ANALYSIS TEST   LEVEL II

Directions to the teacher:

The teacher reads these directions aloud while the children read them silently. Note that there may be more than one answer in a line.

Directions to the children:

Circle the word(s) in each row that indicates more than one (plural).

1. baby   (babies)   baby's   babied
2. cries   cried   (criers)   crying
3. thoughtlessness   rethought   (thoughts)   thoughtful
4. ruler's   ruling   (rulers)   unruled
5. (racers)   raciest   (races)   racing
6. egg   egged   (eggs)   eggs'
7. brush's   (brushes)   brusher   brushing
8. (journeys)   journey's   journied   journey
9. man   manly   (men)   many
10. money   (monies)   money's   monied

Name _____   Grade _____

Directions:

Circle the word(s) in each row that indicates more than one (plural).

1. baby   babies   baby's   babied
2. cries   cried   criers   crying
3. thoughtlessness   rethought   thoughts   thoughtful
4. ruler's   ruling   rulers   unruled
5. racers   raciest   races   racing
6. egg   egged   eggs   eggs'
7. brush's   brushes   brusher   brushing
8. journeys   journey's   journied   journey
9. man   manly   men   many
10. money   monies   money's   monied

STRUCTURAL ANALYSIS TEST   LEVEL III

Directions to the teacher:

Read aloud the directions by each number while the children read them silently.
Note that there may be more than one answer in a line.

1. Circle the words with the affix that means "not."
    a. happiness   (unhappy)   happily   happening
    b. (disoriented)   reoriented   orienting   orienter
    c. (uninterested)   interesting   disinterested   reinterest
    d. (illegal)   legality   leger   legalistic
    e. practical   (impractical)   practically   practice

2. Circle the words with the affix that means "again."
    a. entering   (reenter)   unentered
    b. non-negotiable   negotiate   (renegotiable)

3. Circle the words with the affix that means "against."
    a. freezing   (antifreeze)   frozen
    b. (antisocial)   sociability   society

4. Circle the words with the affix that means "with."
    a. educated   (coeducate)   uneducated
    b. (cooperate)   operating   inoperable

5. Circle the words with the affix that means "before."
    a. paying   payable   (prepaid)
    b. viewed   (preview)   review

Name ——————————   Grade ————

1. Circle the words with the affix that means "not."
   a.   happiness   unhappy   happily   happening
   b.   disoriented   reoriented   orienting   orienter
   c.   uninterested   interesting   disinterested   reinterest
   d.   illegal   legality   leger   legalistic
   e.   practical   impractical   practically   practice
2. Circle the words with the affix that means "again."
   a.   entering   reenter   unentered
   b.   non-negotiable   negotiate   renegotiable
3. Circle the words with the affix that means "against."
   a.   freezing   antifreeze   frozen
   b.   antisocial   sociability   society
4. Circle the words with the affix that means "with."
   a.   educated   coeducate   uneducated
   b.   cooperate   operating   inoperable
5. Circle the words with the affix that means "before."
   a.   paying   payable   prepaid
   b.   viewed   preview   review

STRUCTURAL ANALYSIS TEST   LEVEL IV

Directions to the teacher:

Read these directions aloud while the children read them silently.

Directions to the children:

Underline the suffixes and prefixes in the following words if there are any. Write under the word what the prefix or suffix means. If there is no prefix or suffix, cross the word out.

Sample

unable   dis~~t~~ess
— not

————————   ————————

1. dis~~t~~ict   6. disconnect   11. discomfort
                             not   not
    ————————   ————————   ————————

2. uncouple   7. restart   12. nonpoisonous
    not   again   not
    ————————   ————————   ————————

3. careless   8. unglue   13. re~~li~~sh
    without   not
    ————————   ————————   ————————

4. retell   9. countless   14. co~~u~~ntry
    again   without
    ————————   ————————   ————————

5. postwar   10. anti~~ci~~pate   15. prepaid
    after   before
    ————————   ————————   ————————

H= 90% Correct
M= 80% Correct
L= Below 70% Correct

STUDENTS	Blending		Syllabication				Structural Analysis													
	I	II	I	II	III	IV	I	II	III	IV										

89

Directions:

Underline the suffixes and prefixes in the following words if there are any. write under the word what the prefix or suffix means. If there is no prefix or suffix, cross the word out.

Sample

unable   dis⨉ess
—
  not

_____   _____

1.	district	6.	disconnect	11.	discomfort
2.	uncouple	7.	restart	12.	nonpoisonous
3.	careless	8.	unglue	13.	relish
4.	retell	9.	countless	14.	country
5.	postwar	10.	anticipate	15.	prepaid

SUMMARY

As the teacher administers the tests in this section she will find it useful to note the children's different modes of phonics recognition. The primary channel for recognition of sound-letter relationships can be either the ear or the eye. Both modes are useful, and some children appear to function better in one than the other. Particularly high performance in one type of test and lower performance in the other for a particular child will indicate that appropriate teaching methods or practice work will benefit him more.

Some children, for instance, learn better by seeing a "clue word or letter" and then recognizing a similarity between a sound in that word and sounds in other words. Examples of this approach are found in level I of the alphabet recognition test and level III of the syllabication test. Other children may respond and learn more with teaching techniques that present words or exercises visually. The learning modality test in chapter 3 provides data on this point.

Children who can hear a word and recognize it as being similar *in some part* to the word in print may have a higher score on a test such as level II of the syllabication test. These scores could indicate that the child will respond better to teaching techniques that emphasize listening and responding orally. Recognizing the primary modality used in each test can thus provide a clue for the teacher.

Authorities believe that the accuracy and extent of phonics skills is highly important in developing fluent and accurate reading. For that reason, these tests are among the most important in the series and should be of particular value to the classroom teacher.

SIX

The Assessment
of Oral Reading

Oral reading is a combination of the decoding of words and the attachment of meaning to those words. It can therefore be accepted as one evidence that reading is, in fact, taking place. However, the oral pronunciation of words should not be considered as the complete reading act but rather as one of many ways this act may be observed. Oral reading allows us directly to observe the child applying his acquired reading skills, and in this manner it can be utilized as a valuable diagnostic tool.

If the written word is seen as talk-in-print, as some linguists do, then oral reading takes on great significance. But if the printed word is seen as a means of transmitting meaning that may or may not ever be spoken, then oral reading becomes one of the many ways to utilize print. The process of oral reading can be viewed as a temporary means of achieving some initial objective, such as helping to determine reading level or pronunciation ability, or as a process akin to an art form. As such it is of interest to many but is demanded of few outside the classroom. It has been suggested that only a small portion of the words printed are ever actually pronounced by anyone and that the value of these unpronounced words lies much more in the individual reader's interpretation of the meaning than in the author's intention.

Our point of view is that oral reading is not an integral part of a continuum in the development of reading skills. Rather it is but one of many ways of utilizing the language of the printed page. As such, though it is an instructionally useful step in the acquisition of reading skills, it is neither a prerequisite to nor an essential part of the development of the other reading skills.

Oral reading offers a number of advantages to the teacher in the beginning stages of learning to read. It assists the teacher in helping the child associate printed words and the thought units represented by those words. It assists the child by giving him confirmation of his interpretations of the words, and when he is successful it may give him a sense of having accomplished an important task.

Oral reading brings to the printed word the dimension of variation in tone and emphasis. This aspect of comprehension is more difficult to assess than silent reading. The variation of phrasing and intonation patterns in a given passage can radically change the meaning of what is read, as in the example:

"What are we having for dinner, Stew?"
"What are we having for dinner—stew?"

It is this last step that provides both an opportunity and a dilemma for the teacher of reading. On one hand, creative and divergent renderings of an oral passage can be a stimulating and valuable experience for both students reading orally and audiences listening to the interpretations. On the other hand, teaching for a particularly desired or "expected" emphasis pattern can be most frustrating, as there are numerous instances in which few clues to "correct" pronunciations are provided. This intriguing problem accounts for the many variations and interpretations of literature that abound in the theater. These should be kept in mind when children offer different interpretations of materials read.

LIMITATIONS OF ORAL READING

Oral reading is emphasized in most reading programs. It provides the teacher with evidence of the child's accomplishment or lack of it. Such skills as word pronunciation and use of punctuation can be verified in this way, thereby giving the teacher information that can be useful in planning instruction. Oral reading in the presence of the teacher and a group of peers, a practice sometimes called round-robin reading, may be advantageous for some children in the early stages of reading training. While the concept of "a word" is being developed and strengthened, reading in a group may help them see the correspondence between the spoken and the written word.

Oral reading may be overused in the classroom, however, consuming an unnecessarily large share of the time allotted to reading instruction. It must also be remembered that the round-robin approach can be a psychological problem for the child. It calls the attention of the entire group to an individual and his reading skills or, worse, his lack of them. Either as an initial exposure or as a review, the learner is "on the spot" a few minutes at a time; the rest of his time he observes his classmates while he supposedly follows along silently. Often this becomes merely day dreaming or "get into trouble" time.

Psychologists and learning theorists have generally acknowledged that one of the most important reinforcements in the classroom setting is the relationship of a child to his peer group. When a child or any individual is called on to perform to an audience whose opinions and goodwill are im-

portant in his life, he does so with a certain amount of anxiety and concern. Acceptance by the group is highly important to him. If he is unsuccessful in his performance, the resulting tension and embarrassment may well have undesirable effects. A child whose skills are less well developed than those of others in his peer group can become virtually paralyzed.

Should this situation continue for some time, the child will in many instances learn to defend himself against his feelings of inadequacy by behaving in a way that clearly tells others that reading is not important. He may well come to believe this himself. For such a child, individual oral reading in a group setting may well do more to develop negative attitudes than any other single classroom practice. Oddly enough, frequently the children who comprise the lower half of their class in reading ability are asked to read orally more often than those in the upper half. If positive attitudes toward reading and toward school in general are thought to be important, individual oral reading in a group setting should be minimized.

Excessive use of oral reading can even be a problem for the more capable readers in the classroom. Inattention and boredom are poor reading companions, and certain practices seem to encourage these habits. For example, assigning oral reading to one child after another in order around the reading circle lets the child figure out quickly which part of the text he will be likely to read and reduces his attention to other parts of the lesson. Having each child read the same number of lines or paragraphs usually has the same effect.

Oral reading before silent reading is another practice that can cause the child difficulty, since it ignores the fact that he must perceive and decode the words before he can attack their pronunciation.

The child may develop the habit of reading one word at a time rather than seeing words in blocks or units. The word remains the unit of thought, not the phrase or sentence. Word calling—that is, the correct but labored pronunciation of a long list of words (the sentence) in a relatively meaningless stream—can frequently be found where the program emphasizes oral reading. Teachers may praise clearly and correctly pronounced words, even though such pronunciation reduces the speed of reading material and produces artificial units of thought. Word calling and lack of proper phrasing are habit patterns that can handicap the student.

Another serious drawback of the over-use of oral reading circles is that it significantly reduces the potential rate of reading. The oral reading pace becomes the only reading pace. Many children who may be capable of reading more rapidly develop a habit of reading slowly, since this is the only practice they follow in a reinforcing situation, one in which the teacher may praise them. While accuracy in reading is certainly important, careful oral reading may encourage its development at the expense of flexibility of both purpose and rate.

English and most other languages are highly redundant—that is, their users commonly employ more words, especially such devices as "the" and "a," than are necessary to convey the meaning. In addition, languages have well-used groups of words that are remembered as such—for instance, "quick as a wink." Considerable research suggests that children, when shown an unfamiliar passage from which 20 percent of the words are deleted, can replace more than half the missing words. Anyone who wishes to increase his reading flexibility must learn to identify the key words in a paragraph and to recognize the less important words and phrases for what they are.

Therefore sufficient practice in methods other than oral reading is an important part of the reading program. Particularly in the upper elementary grades, the identification of more and less important words needs to be developed and the reading-learning process streamlined. Individual oral reading in group settings tends to ignore this skill to the point where it ceases to encourage the development of sound and useful reading habits.

USES OF ORAL READING

We do not suggest that oral reading does not have numerous legitimate uses in the classroom. The reading of plays, poetry, and other significant materials that were designed for oral presentation is a most valid and highly useful activity. The expression through voice modulation of intricate shades of meaning is the sole province of the orally read passage and as such contributes a depth and richness to language that no other form of reading does. These legitimate uses of oral reading, with their limited but very important roles in the acquisition of reading skills, can be highly motivating and meaningful for children.

A teacher can place children in temporary groups for instruction in oral reading with a specific purpose. For example, volunteers who will perform in a play might profitably be asked to read lines orally while instruction focuses on the proper stress, pitch, and juncture of their lines. In the same manner, children who need work in oral reading —of poetry, for instance—might be grouped temporarily for that purpose. The reading of poetry can be greatly enhanced by the choral verse method, and the different uses of the voice can be exemplified to the child in such a way that he is involved but does not feel the weight of adverse peer group opinion. Small groups or individuals who have rehearsed well and have been urged to use innovative reading styles in poetry not only can share their understanding with others but can encourage them to become similarly involved.

For children who are shy and have a difficult time expressing themselves even in small groups, the use of puppets and marionettes with a written script can be a valuable instructional tool. In this case, as in the reading of plays, the expressive use of stress, pitch, and juncture can provide the most retiring child with valuable ways to develop his oral language skills in conjunction with his reading skills.

Finally, the description of the skills related to reading and the affective domain would not be complete without reference to the importance of speaking well in a group, large or small. Certainly, oral reading skill developed through some or all of the methods described here will be beneficial in numerous ways. This means of self-expression can be invaluable in providing opportunities for giving recognition and building self-confidence.

TESTS OF ORAL READING

As a tool for the assessment of reading ability, oral reading inventories can be most useful. Particularly at the outset of the school year, an oral reading test is important to the teacher in gaining first-hand knowledge of the child's skills in this area. The correct pronunciation of words provides evidence of visual perception and decoding skills. The reading of short paragraphs also provides a means of checking the speed of reading and skill in phrasing, recognition of punctuation, and tone. Questions after reading give the teacher important information concerning the child's ability to comprehend what he reads.

Oral reading inventories are generally of two types. The first type, sometimes called a quick assessment, consists of lists of words chosen from graded word lists. The child reads the lists from the primary level, for example, and if he makes no errors it is likely that he can read primary material. He is then given successively more difficult lists until he misses a predetermined number of words. Then it can be suggested that the child has reached his ceiling or frustration level.

The second type of inventory consists of short paragraphs also graded for difficulty by levels. They furnish information about phrasing, punctuation, and comprehension as well as word recognition.

To gain maximum information on the children's skills, a teacher should administer reading inventories to each child individually and make records of the errors. Usually the quick assessment is given in the first few days of the school year to furnish quick initial information regarding the child's functioning level. Then the oral reading paragraphs can be administered to confirm and extend initial impressions. While information on the child's reading level will prove helpful, even more valuable is an analysis of the types of errors the child makes while reading: Does he ignore punctuation? Does he skip words or guess them using only the beginning sound as a clue? Can he determine what a word should be from the context of the passage he is reading? Does he reverse letter order, perhaps reading "not" for "ton"?

All of these clues can help the teacher in planning instruction or point to difficulties that may require further testing. Thus if the child consistently mixes middle sounds, "mat" for "met" or "nit" for "net," testing for visual acuity or vowel sounding may be

in order. A teacher can also gain evidence on attitude and feelings by observing signs of nervousness or insecurity in the child. Children who are fearful of reading will need special kinds of help. Usually the oral inventory represents a good starting point in the gathering of data on the child's skill development. These tests can also be utilized later to assess the child's progress in oral reading.

It must be emphasized, however, that oral reading tests do not exactly reflect the child's ability to read and comprehend silently. Great gaps can occur between oral and silent reading skills. Oral reading also offers the teacher little indication as to the child's flexibility in rate of reading or his ability to skim, to find particular information, or to utilize headings, illustrations, and graphics to understand the author's meaning. Though some studies have indicated a relatively high correlation between a child's skill in reading aloud and his performance in other related reading tasks, it can by no means be assumed that the child who reads well orally can also read well silently. Neither can we assume that the child who comprehends well in oral reading will do so in silent reading.

It is also possible for a child who reads well silently to do a poor job in an oral reading situation. Many children who have become rapid silent readers will skip words or stumble over pronunciation, since their eyes sweep ahead faster than they can actually say the words. This may be especially true of the upper grade child. Silent reading tests will be discussed in the next chapter.

In the San Diego Quick Assessment of Reading Ability and the oral reading passages developed for this book, the following marking system is recommended. The teacher will probably find that she will need practice, particularly in the paragraphs, before she can mark the errors smoothly. In the paragraphs, omission and substitution of punctuation marks as well as of words should be marked. Naturally other notations may be added as the teacher desires.

Error Marking System

Omission: ~~cat~~ two lines through word

Mispronun-
ciation: ~~cat~~ one line through word

Insertion:	<u>black</u> ∧ cat	write word above, carat below
Substitution:	<u>kitty</u> cat	write word above, waving line below
Reversals:	→ cat	make arrow above word
Refusals with help:	x cat	make x above word
Refusals without help:	xx cat	make double x above word

Research has indicated that there are three reading levels that are valuable to know for choosing appropriate reading materials for a child. The first is his *independent level.* Here the child recognizes 95 percent of the words in a passage and knows the answers to at least 85 percent of the associated comprehension questions. This is the level the child should be encouraged to use in selecting library books and independent skill exercises. This is where he will feel most successful. The next is his *instructional level.* Here the child can read 85 to 90 percent of the words and answer 75 percent of the comprehension questions. This is the level the teacher utilizes when she is working with the child and is available for help with the words he does not know. Any higher percentage of errors than this is described as the child's *frustration level*, which should be avoided for independent or instructional purposes. Some studies have shown that schools require as many as 50 percent of the children tested to read at their frustration level. Such a practice spells defeat and misery for the child. These three levels will be utilized as guidelines for the oral reading tests in this book.

SAN DIEGO QUICK ASSESSMENT OF READING ABILITY

This test consists of thirteen word lists graded from preprimer through junior high. The words within each list are of about the same difficulty. The first five lists can be considered primary level, the next four lists intermediate level, and the last four lists upper level. Typing the words in a column on a four-by-seven-inch index card with the grade level marked on the back is usually the easiest way to prepare the test for administration.

Because the number of words in each list is limited, zero errors is considered independent level, one error instructional level, and two errors frustration level. The teacher should begin with a list two or three sets below the child's presumed functioning level in school (or lower if she feels he has reading difficulties) and have him read the words on each list until he makes two errors. Errors are recorded on a separate sheet that can be prepared in multiple copies.

This separate record sheet can be a rough starting point for initial instruction and further investigation. At this point, it would be appropriate to begin a tentative profile on the child's strengths and weaknesses. Formulation of a tentative hypothesis concerning the child's skills can then be supported or contradicted by additional information to be gathered from such techniques as the assessment of oral paragraph reading.

SAN DIEGO QUICK ASSESSMENT OF READING ABILITY

Directions to the teacher:

Type out each list of ten words on an index card. For primary children, begin with a card that is at level II; for intermediate, level IV; and for upper and secondary, level VI. Ask the student to read the words aloud. If he misreads any on the list, drop to easier lists until he makes no errors. This indicates the base level.

Directions to the children:

Read each list of words. Say each word carefully. Begin.

Analysis of the test:

The list in which a student misses no words is the level at which he can read independently. One error indicates his instructional level. Two or more errors identify the level at which reading material will be too difficult for him.

An analysis of a student's errors is useful. Among those that occur with greatest frequency are the following:

Error	*Examples*
reversal	ton for not
consonant	how for now
consonant clusters	state for straight
short vowel	cane for can
long vowel	wid for wide
prefix	inproved for improved
suffix	improve for improved
miscellaneous	accent, omission of syllables, etc.

As with other reading tasks, the teacher must observe the student's behavior. Such things as posture, facial expression, and voice quality may signal restlessness, lack of assurance, or frustration while reading.

Readiness	2	4	6	8
see	you	road	our	city
play	come	live	please	middle
me	not	thank	myself	moment
at	with	when	town	frightened
run	jump	bigger	early	exclaimed
go	help	how	send	several
and	is	always	wide	lonely
look	work	night	believe	drew
can	are	spring	quietly	since
here	this	today	carefully	straight

10	12	14	16
decided	scanty	bridge	amber
served	certainly	commercial	dominion
amazed	develop	abolish	sundry
silent	considered	trucker	capillary
wrecked	discussed	apparatus	impetuous
improved	behaved	elementary	blight
certainly	splendid	comment	wrest
entered	acquainted	necessity	enumerate
realized	escaped	gallery	daunted
interrupted	grim	relativity	condescend

18	20	22	24
capacious	conscientious	zany	galore
limitation	isolation	jerkin	rotunda
pretext	molecule	nausea	capitalism
intrigue	ritual	gratuitous	prevaricate
delusion	momentous	linear	risible
immaculate	vulnerable	inept	exonerate
ascent	kinship	legality	superannuate
acrid	conservatism	aspen	luxuriate
binocular	jaunty	amnesty	piebald
embankment	inventive	barometer	crunch

SAN DIEGO QUICK ASSESSMENT OF READING ABILITY
SCORE SHEET

Reader _____   Tested by _____

Age _____ Grade _____   Date of Test _____

ERROR TYPE	EXAMPLE	ERROR TYPE	EXAMPLE
reversal	was for saw	long vowel	wid for wide
consonant	now for how	prefix	inproved for improved
consonant cluster	state for straight	suffix	improve for improved
short vowel	cane for can	miscellaneous	accent, ommission of syllables

Card no. _____   Card no. _____   Card no. _____
Errors   Errors   Errors

Card no. _____   Card no. _____   Card no. _____
Errors   Errors   Error

ORAL READING PASSAGES

The next step in the diagnostic process is the use of oral reading passages. In this instrument, the child is asked to read aloud each passage carefully. He should start two levels below the one indicated as instructional on the quick assessment or at the level indicated on the test. The teacher records the errors, omissions, and the like on a separate copy of the same passage and asks the comprehension questions provided for it. A separate card for each passage will prove helpful. If a typewriter with large primary type is available, it should be used for the easier passages.

Because passages vary in length, the number of errors for each level should be calculated on a percentage basis. Percentage figures are given in the directions for the test. The teacher may wish to make note not only of word-by-word errors but also of errors in phrasing and punctuation that suggest the child needs specific skill instruction. Since each set of questions inquires into both literal and interpretive comprehension, children with needs in one of these areas can be identified. At this point, the tentative profile of the quick assessment can be strengthened or modified. The same check sheet used for the quick assessment can be used for these passages.

Oral Reading Check Sheet – Level Attained and Types of Errors

Check (✓) if error noted Leave blank if no error STUDENTS	Independent Level	Instructional Level	Frustration Level	Omission	Mispronunciation	Insertion	Substitution	Reversals	Refusal w/out help	Error in Consonant	Error in Con-sonant Cluster	Error in Short Vowel	Error in Long Vowel	Error in Prefix	Error in Suffix	Accent Error	Punctuation Error				

Directions to the teacher:

There are seven levels in this test. Primary levels are generally II, IV and VI; intermediate, VI, VIII, and X; and upper, X, XII, and XIV.

Ask each child to read the paragraph aloud. On a separate copy of the paragraph, mark the errors he makes as previously described. When the child has finished reading the story, ask him the comprehension questions for that story. Note the number of correct and incorrect responses. Interpretation and evaluation questions do not have answers noted, since many possible replies can be accepted.

As a general rule, start with level II for primary grade children, with level VI for intermediate grade children, and with level X for upper grade and secondary students.

Stop the test when the child makes more than 25 percent oral reading errors or more than 50 percent comprehension errors.

For this material the independent level is 95 percent word recognition, 85 percent comprehension; the instruction level is 85 percent to 90 percent word recognition, 75 percent comprehension.

Directions to the child:

Read this story out loud. When you are through, I will ask you some questions about what you have read. Ready? Begin.

ORAL READING TEST   LEVEL II

"Look here, Bill," said Ann.
"See my ball?"
"It can go fast."
"It can go high."
"I like my ball."

Bill said, "I like your ball, Ann."
"I like your red ball."
"I like my blue ball, too."

(38 words)

Comprehension questions   Level II

1. What can Ann's ball do? (Go fast, go high)
2. What does Ann want Bill to do? (Look at her)
3. How are the balls different? (One is red, one is blue)
4. What do Bill and Ann like to do? (Play ball, play catch, play together, etc.)

ORAL READING TEST   LEVEL IV

Jim was holding a top. "Let me see you spin it," said Jack. Jim made it go very fast. "I wish I had that top," Jack said.

88684

Jack picked it up. "I'll give you this ball for it," he said. "I'll even give you my cowboy hat and my red car, too. Just wait here."

Jack ran into the house. Jack came out with the ball, hat, and car. "You can have this belt, too," he said, as he took it off.

Before Jim could say anything, Jack put the ball, hat, and car in his hands. Jack put the belt in Jim's hand. Jack took the top.

"Have fun with the top," said Jim. "I have another top in my room. I was going to give this one to you, but you didn't give me a chance."

(138 words)

Comprehension questions   *Level IV*

1. What was Jim holding?   (A top)
2. Where did Jack go to get the toys?   (His house)
3. Did Jack get what he wanted?   (Yes)
4. How many things did Jack give Jim?   (Four)
.5. How do you think Jack feels now?

ORAL READING TEST   LEVEL VI

The lifeguard helps people when they are in the water. He is a good swimmer. He is strong and does not get tired quickly. He can swim fast. He must run into the water if someone needs help.

The lifeguard sits on a tower beside the water. He can see well from there. He must be able to see everyone.

Sometimes the lifeguard blows his whistle. If people do not follow the safety rules, the lifeguard talks to them. He explains what they must do to be safe in the water. The lifeguard makes sure that everyone follows the rules.

If the lifeguard sees someone who needs help, he races to the water and dives in. Soon he is at the side of the person who needs help. The lifeguard takes the person and swims back. He must carry the person in the right way. Otherwise, he could be pulled under the water by the frightened person.

On some days the lifeguard is busier than others. On hot days many people come to swim and cool off. Sometimes it is hard for the lifeguard to see all of them. He does his best to keep everyone safe in the water.

(200 words)

Comprehension questions   *Level VI*

1. Who is the story about?   (A lifeguard)
2. Where does a lifeguard sit?   (On a tower)
3. When he sees someone who needs help, what does he do?   (Races to the water and dives in)
4. When is a lifeguard busy?   (On hot days)
5. What might happen if people did not follow the safety rules?

Some of the wild animals that man first tamed were sheep. They have been raised by man for thousands of years. Long ago man discovered that sheep can give him both food and clothing. Some people drink sheep's milk and they make cheese from the milk.

Most sheep are raised on the range. They graze over dry pasture lands and eat grass and other plants. Large numbers are raised in the southwestern part of the United States. Texas has more sheep than any other state. Sheep live in large groups called flocks. A flock may have as many as two thousand sheep. One sheep usually leads the flock. It is usually a male sheep called a ram.

The man who cares for sheep is called a shepherd. He has a dog to help him. The dog keeps the sheep together by circling them. He nips at their heels if they wander too far away. The dog also helps protect the sheep from animals who might hurt them.

By the time sheep are four months old they are big enough to go to market. Meat from young sheep is called lamb. Meat from older sheep is called mutton. Lamb is better than mutton. Most people in the United States like lamb better than mutton.

(212 words)

Comprehension questions   Level VIII

1. What was one of the first animals tamed?   (Sheep)
2. Where are they raised?   (The range)
3. Who cares for these animals?   (A shepherd and his dog)
4. What is the meat from these young animals called?   (Lamb)
5. When they get older, what is the meat called?   (Mutton)
6. Why do you think people like to eat lamb better than mutton?

ORAL READING TEST   LEVEL X

"Master! Me belly walk about too much!" said the islander with a stomach ache. Visitors are not surprised to hear these English words. They recognize them as a form of "pidgin."

Pidgin sounds like "baby-talk." Today it is used by many people and is commonly heard in the islands of the Pacific.

When the Western world began trading with China about 400 years ago, traders needed to talk to each other. However, they were not able to learn each other's language. A baby-talk form of English, with a few Chinese words added, was developed. It was known as "business language." But when the Chinese said business, it sounded like pidgin.

Pidgin was used by sailors who stopped at the South Pacific islands. The natives had learned pidgin from the British sailors.

Pidgin varies from place to place because it is a combination of English and the native language. But it is always a simple language with about 1,000 words. It is a useful language. In a short time a native can learn enough pidgin to hold a job. English speaking people are learning pidgin. They know that the natives will understand the words "Me friend."

(198 words)

1. What does pidgin sound like?   (Baby-talk)
2. Pidgin was first a mixture of what two languages?   (English and Chinese)
3. How was pidgin brought to the Pacific islands?   (By sailors)
4. About how many words are there in pidgin?   (1,000)
5. What use is made of pidgin?   (In trading and among people who speak different languages)
6. Why was it important for the people to communicate?
7. Why is trade with other countries necessary?

ORAL READING TEST   LEVEL XII

It's hard to decide what to watch when you attend an outdoor track meet. On a flat, grass-covered athletic field, contestants are involved in jumping and throwing events. On an oval cinder path around the field, runners are competing. To the sports-minded, a track meet is as spellbinding as a science fiction adventure.

For many, the track events are the most exciting. There is always an abundance of action. If you attend a good-sized track meet, chances are you would see 100-yard and 220-yard dashes, and 440-yard, 880-yard, and 1-mile races.

When ten hurdle fences are put on the track the hurdle races begin. In the hurdle races, the runners jump over these fences. There are two kinds of hurdle races. In low-hurdle races, the fences are 2½ feet high. Fences 3 or 3½ feet high are used in high-hurdle races. The length of a race determines the distance between the hurdles. They may be 10 to 40 feet apart.

In the relay races teams of four men compete. All racers run the same distance. The first man on all competing teams begins running at the sound of the gun. Each runner carries a small baton or rod. As he completes his lap, he passes the baton to the next runner on his team. Men who race the final lap are called anchor men. Anchor men are usually the fastest runners.

(241 words)

Comprehension questions   *Level XII*

1. How long are dashes?   (100, 220 yards)
2. What kinds of hurdle fences are there?   (Low and high)
3. How many men are there on a relay team?   (4)
4. Who is the last man on a relay team?   (The anchor man)
5. How would you describe a track meet?   (Exciting, spellbinding)
6. Describe the place where track meets are held.   (Grass-covered athletic fields with an oval cinder track)
7. What is usually used to start a race?   (A gun)
8. Why do people enjoy watching track meets?

West Germany is located in central Europe. It is bordered by Denmark, Switzerland, Austria, Czechoslovakia, and East Germany. The Netherlands, Belgium, Luxembourg, and France also border West Germany. The northern shores of West Germany are washed by the cold waters of the North and Baltic seas. West Germany is the home of fifty million prosperous people.

Much of West Germany's industrial strength is based on the supply of minerals within the soil. West Germany's coal deposits are the most important in western Europe. The Nation's outstanding coalfields are found in the Ruhr and the Saar regions. Despite being favored by rich deposits of coal, potash, and rock salt, the areas must import some minerals, largely iron ore.

West Germany has had amazing economic growth in the years following World War II. Though left in ruins at the end of the war, today it is an industrial giant. Huge mills produce a stream of steel. Metal objects varying from knives to automobiles come from factories. Chemicals and textiles are products of major importance. West German workers take pride in making articles that require their skill. West German cameras, watches, and precision instruments are among the world's finest. Their capitalist system has produced one of the strongest economies in the world.

(209 words)

Comprehension questions   Level XIV

1. How many people live in West Germany?   (Fifty million)
2. On what is West Germany's industrial strength based?   (Minerals in the soil)
3. What kind of economic growth has West Germany made?   (Rapid)
4. What was it like in Germany at the end of World War II?   (Left in ruins)
5. How do West Germans feel about their products?   (Proud)
6. How good are West German manufactured goods?   (Among the finest in the world)
7. What are the features of a capitalist economy?
8. Is capitalism a good system?

SUMMARY

It is important to group those children together for instruction whose oral reading profiles reflect a specific skill need. This saves the time of the teacher, since she need not repeat instruction where it is unnecessary. It also tends to speed the child's progress. The group can be disbanded after each child has mastered the particular skill.

It is equally important to have the child's reading material reflect, as nearly as possible, his correct independent and instructional level. These assessments should make this possible.

SEVEN

The Assessment of Silent Reading

From an instructional point of view, oral reading would appear to be a logical means of identifying a child's reading skills. Print, however, must be decoded silently before it can be read orally. Therefore oral reading can be viewed as simply an extension of silent reading skills. If we look at reading as a communication process, we can begin to get a different view of the purposes of reading. Rather than merely "talk written down," which implies the need for oral reproduction, the author of a passage can be thought of as a sender and the reader as a receiver. The print, then, provides a medium from which the receiver selects and interprets material to suit his own purposes as he decodes the printed word.

The communication process can provide a great deal of information for reception and interpretation. The reading process, in these terms, requires thinking critically, selecting, and evaluating as well as decoding words. It is this view which suggests that reading for information forms the core of subject matter teaching.

DECODING AND SILENT READING

Shortly after the child learns to recognize print as representative of language and gains a vocabulary of approximately 100 words,

effective and useful silent reading skills begin, in many cases, to develop. When the child reads silently, he has the opportunity to gain information in a slightly different way from when he is reading orally. The pronunciation task, which is difficult for some children, does not necessarily interfere with the child's understanding of the words or his ability to decode them as such. How many times has a child behaved as if he understood the word but was unable to pronounce it? It may be that sometimes the pronunciation of the word, the physical making of the sounds appropriate to the printed symbols, slows him down or stops him when, if he were reading silently, he could continue without interruption.

Of equal importance in the silent reading process is the ability of the child to receive messages from the author directly without interference from his immediate environment. Neither the teacher nor other children participate directly in a child's silent reading or are aware of it in the way they are of oral reading. This feature of silent reading tends to personalize the relationship between the author and the reader. This personalization can be utilized in the classroom to motivate readers and to encourage children to spend a considerable amount of time living vicariously through the words of other children, animals, and fantasy characters in the worlds of the past and future as well as the present. Perhaps by not requiring the oral reading task we can introduce the child to scenes far beyond the world of the classroom. It may be that this will encourage reading and stimulate his imagination and creative thought in countless ways.

SILENT READING AND FLEXIBILITY OF RATE

Silent reading, unlike oral reading, is not tied to the physical process of producing words and need not be related to any movement of the throat muscles. Readers thus can develop the ability to vary their reading rates selectively.

It is unfortunate that in many classrooms emphasis on oral reading precludes the development of the habits of varying comprehension and rate, which should be learned early in the reading program. The results of this are countless thousands of young people who, even in college, read at the rate of 200 to 250 words per minute regardless of the material.

It may be well to emphasize at this point that the reading rate is only one factor that affects comprehension and appreciation. Such factors as print size, number and type of illustrations, style, and kind of subject matter also have a profound effect. Many childern will struggle with a "difficult" book even though they must read it extremely slowly if their interest is sufficiently aroused. In discussing individual flexibility in reading, silent reading must be considered a most important tool.

SILENT READING AND THE STUDY SKILLS

The identification of pertinent information in a passage is a vital part of a child's ability to use the printed word in pursuit of solutions to problems or as a source of information. Outlining, summarizing, and identifying key concepts and key words in prose and poetry, are often the central focus of classroom instruction no matter what subject is being considered. It is therefore most important for the elementary school teacher to do all she can from the earliest stages to help her children develop the study skills as-

sociated with silent reading. If students can find a key word or phrase on a page of printed material, separate the unimportant from the vital issues, comprehend various levels of information, and vary the reading rate and approach for the material at hand, they will be well equipped for future reading tasks.

TESTING FOR SILENT READING COMPREHENSION

There are two major approaches to testing for silent reading comprehension. These are Graded Silent Reading Paragraphs with comprehension questions and Cloze Reading Tests in which words are systematically deleted by the teacher and are then replaced by the student (Bornently, 1964). Both have particular advantages and disadvantages for the classroom.

Graded reading paragraphs are a series of paragraphs of increasing difficulty. The child reads a paragraph, then the teacher asks him comprehension questions. If the teacher gives the paragraphs to a group of children she may also provide answer sheets. If she gives the test individually the reading may also be timed or untimed at her discretion. Following each of the paragraphs is a set of questions that fall into three types: literal, interpretive, and inferential.

The graded reading paragraphs have inherent strengths that have made their use widespread for many years. These strengths include ease of administration, their ability to tap different levels of comprehension, and the information they provide regarding the rate of reading.

Because these tests can be administered to large groups under usual classroom circumstances, they reduce the amount of time and effort associated with individual testing such as the oral paragraphs require. The directions for completing the tests are easily understood, particularly if the answers to the comprehension questions are multiple-choice in format. This format also makes scoring a simple, one-step operation.

The potential for tapping different levels of comprehension can be most beneficial. It is possible for the teacher to add levels of comprehension beyond those included if it suits the needs of her class. Translation, the ability to use synonyms; evaluation, the ability to make value judgments; and synthesis, the ability to arrive at new solutions, can all be drawn from reading the paragraph. But since evaluation and synthesis are more subjective levels of comprehension and do not imply only one answer, these types of questions must be asked on an individual basis. Assessing the reading rate also requires individual or small group administration since the teacher must keep an accurate record of the time required to finish reading.

In spite of these strengths, some notable weaknesses of using silent reading paragraphs should be kept in mind. The greatest is the teacher's problem in analyzing the causes of incorrect responses. It is frequently difficult to determine from the examination or even by individual questioning whether failure to comprehend the paragraph or the question caused an incorrect response. And there may be other reasons. There is the problem of prior knowledge, for example. How can a teacher be sure that the information is novel for a particular child? After all, if he already knows the material, he may be able to answer the questions without reading the passage at all. Then, too, a child who may be able to comprehend the passage and the questions may get a lower score because he is unfamiliar with the test procedure itself. Young children who are not familiar with the multiple-choice format are particularly likely to get lower scores than those who are. Because of these difficulties, information from these tests (as with all testing instruments) should be used to generate hunches or hypotheses regarding a particular child's difficulties rather than accepted as definitive and valid.

The second instrument used to assess silent reading comprehension is the cloze test. This approach, which was developed within the last twenty years, has been extensively utilized as a technique in teaching and readability research and to determine a child's ability to comprehend printed material. The test itself is relatively easy to construct and score.

The most commonly used procedure is to select a passage of about 250 words that is novel for the child. Every fifth word is then deleted and replaced by a blank of a standard length. The child is given the passage with directions to fill in as many blanks as he can with the word he thinks the author

intended. The child must write in the exact word and not a synonym for the answer to be considered correct, even if the alternative makes sense. The interpretation of the scores (or percentage of correct answers) obtained has been the subject of considerable research. If 44 percent of the answers are correct, this score appears to be equivalent to a 75 percent score on a conventional multiple-choice comprehension test. This score represents the *instructional level* discussed in chapter 6. The *independent level* of 90 percent on a multiple choice test is equivalent to 55 percent on a cloze test.

Those who have used the cloze test maintain that this technique taps more than "comprehension" levels. They see the test as defining the reading act by measuring the degree to which the language patterns of the author and the reader coincide. Using this definition of reading, it may be possible to measure how well a child understands any material we wish to use in the curriculum, whether or not we have "grading" information on it.

It is often difficult for a teacher to assess the appropriateness of books and other reading materials. Can a given group really use the regular social studies or science book? Are the other materials, such as magazines or supplementary books, within the child's range of ability? Can children who speak a particular dialect follow the ideas and sentence patterns of a book written in standard English? Because the child determines the missing words from the context, cultural language patterns, prior information, and the shades of meaning of other words all contribute to the child's performance. All these factors determine whether a child will really understand and be able to learn from the materials he is given. If we utilize the same comprehension levels as the oral reading paragraphs, it is possible to determine what materials are appropriate for our classes. In this way the cloze technique can be highly useful for the classroom teacher.

Another factor that should not be overlooked is the child's reaction to cloze tests. Most children find them challenging and fun—a puzzle rather than a test. This makes their frequent use possible without the children's becoming frustrated. The advantages of a cloze test are that it is easy to prepare and score, considers many factors of reading comprehension beyond the scope of the multiple-choice test, and assesses widely differing materials for classroom use.

The cloze test also has some disadvantages. It does not give the teacher data related to different levels of comprehension—literal, interpretive, and inferential items cannot be separated, as they can in the multiple-choice test. The scoring of a cloze test also necessarily involves a judgmental factor. Children's spelling errors may influence the decision on the answer's correctness. Thus a child who has poor spelling skills may receive a lower cloze score than one with equal reading comprehension ability but better spelling skills.

SILENT READING PARAGRAPHS

There are seven graded reading paragraphs included in this test. These range from primary to upper grade levels. The earlier paragraphs cannot usually be successfully administered to primary children until they have acquired sufficient vocabulary and skill to read short passages independently. Note that some rebus techniques are used at this level to supplement existing vocabulary—for example:

The  is red.

After each paragraph there are several comprehension questions. Lower level paragraphs have four questions, and intermediate and upper level paragraphs have more. This feature makes calculation of the 75 percent instructional comprehension level relatively easy.

The first type of question is one requiring literal comprehension or memory—that is, comprehension of the material as presented in the selection read. For example:

The sky was cloudy and the wind was starting to blow hard.

Johnny's mother called him into the house.

The above selection could have literal comprehension questions like the following:

What did the sky look like?

How was the wind blowing?

The exact words used in the paragraph are the answers to the literal comprehension questions. The interpretive questions, on the other hand, ask the child to extract directly what the paragraph is saying. For example, based on the paragraph above:

Johnny's mother probably called him into the house because:

1. it was too hot
2. it was too windy
3. it was time for bed

In this instance of interpretation, the exact words in the paragraph may or may not be used but the child is asked to determine, from the information given: (1) why the actions or events happened (2) what the motives were that may have moved events in the direction they took, or (3) similar applications of reasoning to explain the events.

In inferential comprehension, the child is asked to extend the actual events of the story in time and space. For example:

In the paragraph above is it most likely that:

1. a storm was coming up
2. there was going to be an earthquake
3. Johnny's mother was cooking dinner

In this instance, the child is asked to utilize the information gained first to determine what is and is not relevant. Second, based on the information he is asked to develop hypotheses regarding what the surrounding implied circumstances are, were, or may become. Questions can be asked orally or presented in written form.

Two minutes are allowed to read each paragraph. If the child cannot complete the paragraph in that time, his reading rate is probably too slow and this should be noted. Once the questions have been scored, one child's score can easily be compared with his previous scores or class averages. The latter practice is recommended only under special circumstances, such as when instructional materials or procedures are being evaluated. We do not recommend comparing one child's progress with that of another for evaluation purposes.

Directions to the teacher:

Each paragraph should be on a separate page. Questions and answers may be prepared in a multiple-choice format, if desired. Suggested beginning levels are: primary, level II; intermediate, level IV; upper, level VI.

Give an individual or a small group of children the paragraphs they are to read. Allow not more than two minutes for reading the selection. Then have the children turn the page face down and answer the questions in writing as you dictate them. For immature boys and girls, individual administration with oral responses to questions may be necessary.

Directions to the children:

Read the story carefully to yourself. When you have finished you may reread the story if you have time. I will stop you in two minutes and ask you some questions about what you have read. Ready? Begin.

Silent Reading Paragraphs   Level A

"Look at these [flowers], Mother," said Jane.

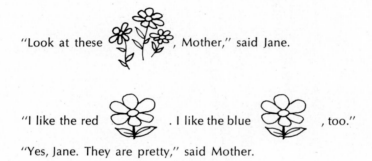

"I like the red [flower]. I like the blue [flower], too."

"Yes, Jane. They are pretty," said Mother.

"Come in the [house], Jane.

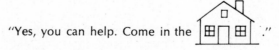

We will look at the [flowers] later."

"Can I help, Mother?" said Jane.

"Yes, you can help. Come in the [house]."

Memory

1. What does Jane like?   (Flowers)
2. What colors are the flowers?   (Red and blue)

Inference

3. Where are Mother and Jane?   (Outside)

Interpretation

4. Why does Jane want to help?

SILENT READING PARAGRAPHS   LEVEL II

Mother looked at the cat and dog. "Come in the house," she said. The black and white dog and the yellow cat came running into the house.

Soon Dick and Mary ran home. School was out. They got in the car with little Bill and Mother. The dog and cat got in the car. Away they went. Soon they came to the big store. All of them went in.

Mother looked at a red coat. Dick looked at some toys. Mary looked at the books. There were many things to look at. No one looked at little Bill.

Soon it came time to go home. "Where is little Bill?" said Mother. "I don't see him." Mother went looking. Dick and Mary went looking.

They walked past the toys and coats. They walked past the books and tables and chairs. They came to the beds. "Look!" said Dick. There were little Bill and the dog and cat asleep.

Memory

1. What did Mary look at in the store?   (Books)
2. What had happened to Bill?   (He was asleep)

Inference

3. Do Bill, Dick, and Mary like animals?   (Yes) How do you know?

Interpretation

4. How does Bill feel?

SILENT READING PARAGRAPHS   LEVEL IV

A waiter works in a restaurant. He asks people what they want to eat. He brings people many kinds of food.

When people come in he gives them a menu. It tells what food the restaurant has. It also tells how much the food costs. After the people look over the menu, they tell the waiter what they want to eat. The waiter takes their order.

The waiter carries the order to the cook. He gets the food ready, then he gives it to the waiter. The waiter puts it on a tray. He then takes it to the table.

As the people eat, the waiter checks to see that they have the things they need. Sometimes he brings more water, milk, or coffee. When the people have finished eating the waiter clears the table. He finds out what they want for dessert. The waiter gets the dessert for them.

Memory

1. What is the first thing a waiter gives the people?   (Menu)
2. What is on the menu?   (The food the restaurant has and its price)
3. What does the waiter do when the people are through eating?   (Clears the table)
4. What does the waiter bring to the table after the people have been served? (Water, milk, coffee)

5. How does a waiter try to please his customers? (By serving them in many different ways)

Interpretation

6. What qualities does a waiter need?

SILENT READING PARAGRAPHS   LEVEL VI

Cattle are raised for their meat and their milk. The meat is called beef. We eat beef more than other meat.

Beef cattle are raised on ranches. A number of cattle is a herd. Herds of cattle feed on grass land. Sometimes they are fed hay. When the cattle are ready they are sent to a stockyard.

A stockyard is where animals are kept until they are sold. In the stockyards the cattle are fattened on corn. Corn-fed cattle give rich quality beef. Buyers visit the stockyards and choose the animals they want. Buyers know how to judge the quality of meat in every animal.

From the stockyards the cattle are sent to a packing plant in trains and trucks. In the packing plant the animals are killed. Some of the meat is put in cans but most is kept fresh.

Memory

1. A number of cattle together is called —————. (Herd)
2. Where are cattle kept until sold? (Stockyard)
3. How do cattle go to the packing plants? (In trains and trucks)
4. What happens to meat that is not kept fresh? (Put in cans)

Inference

5. What do cattle buyers look for in the animals they buy? (Health, good weight)

Interpretation

6. Why are cattle important?

SILENT READING PARAGRAPHS   LEVEL VIII

Muir wanted to explore a glacier that was between two mountain peaks. He and his partner left their camp on the east side of the mountain. They climbed higher through heaps of fallen logs. They reached the edge of the ice river and spiked their way to the top of the glacier. They crossed to the west side, jumping over each crevasse. On the west side they saw the edge of a forest. They turned north until they came to a huge crevasse. This led into a lake, which was full of floating ice. On the return trip they crossed one crevasse only to face a larger one. They were caught standing on an island in the ice. They crossed the large crevasse by crawling across an ice bridge and from there back to camp.

Memory

1. What did Muir want to explore? (A glacier)
2. How did they get to the top of the glacier? (Spiked their way up)
3. What was in the lake? (Floating ice)

4. On the return trip where were they caught? (On an island of ice)

Inference

5. What is a crevasse? (A deep crack in the ice)

Interpretation

6. Why did they want to explore the glacier?

SILENT READING PARAGRAPHS   LEVEL X

On June 14 of 1777, the Continental Congress—the governing body of the colonies—decided that the official flag of the colonies should be thirteen stripes alternating red and white, with a blue rectangle at the upper left-hand corner of the flag in which there were thirteen stars, white on a blue field.

The Congress did not prescribe an official arrangement for the stars, so several designs appeared. One designer arranged all thirteen stars in a circle. Another put twelve stars in a circle with the thirteenth in the center.

No one knows who designed the first flag, nor did the Continental Congress leave any record of why it chose red, white, and blue as the colors for the flag. Perhaps it is because the flag grew up around the British flag, which carried those same colors.

The next change in the flag came in 1794 with the admission of two new states. The flag was altered to have fifteen stars and fifteen stripes—a star and stripe for each state. The stars were displayed in five rows of three stars each.

Memory

1. What group decided on the first flag of the colonies? (Continental Congress)
2. What part of the flag did they fail to prescribe? (Arrangement of the stars)
3. Who designed the first flag? (No one knows)
4. Why were red, white, and blue chosen as the colors? (Perhaps because they were used in the British flag)

Inference

5. How was the flag designed so that it might be changed as states were added? (Stars and stripes could be added)
6. Why was more than one designer used? (To obtain a variety of ideas for the best final decision)

Interpretation

7. Why did the new country want a flag?

SILENT READING PARAGRAPHS   LEVEL XII

Many of the animals we normally associate with Africa are found in Ethiopia. Monkeys and baboons abound in many regions. The elephant and the rhinoceros are seen in widespread areas. Hippopotamuses and crocodiles inhabit lakes and rivers. Snakes are common. Lions are found in parts of the country. Leopards found there are unusually large. Fierce hyenas are everywhere, even in the nation's capital city!

The nation's capital, Addis Ababa, lies eight thousand feet above sea level. The city has a population of half a million people. The high elevation of the city gives its residents a cool climate. Modern buildings, a hospital, a library, a museum, and a university have been built. Three miles from the city a modern airfield links Ethiopia to other countries.

Memory

1. What is our impression of animals found in Ethiopia? (They are normally associated with Africa)
2. What two animals in particular inhabit the lakes and rivers? (Hippopotamuses and crocodiles)
3. How are leopards and hyenas described? (Leopards are large and hyenas are fierce)
4. How many people live in Addis Ababa? (Half a million)

Inference

5. What makes Addis Ababa a desirable place to live? (Cool climate, modern buildings, and transportation)
6. In what ways has Ethiopia modernized her capital? (Modern buildings, airport, university, etc.)

Interpretation

7. Why do you think Addis Ababa is the capital city?

CLOZE READING TESTS

Six passages are included for use as cloze tests. As in the other silent tests, children below the latter half of first grade or the beginning of second grade will probably not be able to utilize this test because of a lack of both reading and spelling skills. However, at this or any level the teacher can construct cloze tests based on the material being used in the classroom provided the children have not already read it.

CLOZE TESTS

Directions to the teacher:

Read the instructions to the children aloud while the children read them silently. Allow the children as much time as needed to complete all blanks.

Levels 1 and 2 can be considered primary Levels; Levels 3 and 4 are intermediate Levels; and Levels 5 and 6 are upper Levels.

Directions to the children:

Write only one word in each blank. Try to fill in every blank. Don't be afraid to guess. Wrong spelling will not count against you if we can tell what you mean. Are there any questions? You may begin.

Cloze Exercise   Level I

"Look in the garden," _____ Bill. "There is something _____ _____ there. Some thing is walking _____ in there. It looks _____ a little puppy."

Just _____ a little animal came _____ of the garden. It _____ black with white down _____ back. It had a _____ tail. "Let's make a _____ out of it," said _____.

"I'll get it some _____," said Jim. He went _____ the house. His Uncle _____ him come in. "Don't _____ anything now," he said." _____ are going to eat _____ soon."

"This milk isn't _____ me," said Jim. "It's _____ our new pet. Bill _____ I have a new _____. It's out in the _____ yard. You will like _____. Take a look."

Uncle _____ out the back door. "_____!" he said. "Oh, no. _____ away from it, Bill. _____ away from it. It's _____ a pet. It's a _____!"

Cloze Exercise   Level II

The zoo keeper has _____ job that many children _____ like to have. His _____ seems like play. Most _____ like animals. The zoo _____ likes many animals, too, _____ he has to work _____ to take care of _____.

Every day the zoo _____ must feed all the _____. This is more work _____ getting dinner ready for _____ big family. At home, _____ eats the same food. _____ the zoo, all the _____ do not get the _____ thing to eat.

He _____ hard to keep the _____ clean. The animals must _____ washed. Some animals need _____. The cages must be _____. The floor must be _____.

The zoo keeper knows _____ lot about animals. Children _____ him many questions. Some _____ to know all about _____. Some want to know _____ to feed the bears. _____ want to know how _____ make a parrot talk.

The zoo keeper likes _____ and girls to come _____ the zoo. He has _____ watching them with the _____.

Cloze Exercise   Level III

Many _____ live in the sea. _____ these are fish. They _____ a bone that goes _____ their backs. It is _____ a backbone. They may _____ through openings in the _____ of their bodies which _____ called gills. Fish have _____ rather than thick skin. _____ of arms and legs, _____ have fins which often _____ them balance and swim.

_____ are two big groups _____ fish. They are the _____ fish and the fresh _____ fish. Fish which live _____ the ocean are called _____-water fish. Often these _____ are blue gray in _____. Fish which come from _____ and lakes where the _____ is without salt are _____ fresh-water fish. They _____ usually brownish-green or _____-green in color.

Another _____ of sea animals is _____ the shellfish. They are _____ really fish at all. _____ be true fish they

_____ have to have a _____. Shellfish live in or _____ _____ the water, however, and _____ covered with a shell _____ protects their bodies.

Cloze Exercise   Level IV

Before ancient man could _____ a real hunter, there _____ _____ something he had to _____. He had to find _____ _____ how fire could be _____ as a tool. Without _____ _____ help of fire, Ancient _____ could not eat with _____ animals. With his pointed _____ he could spear rabbits _____ mice, but he could _____ cook them. All animals _____ hunt have sharp teeth _____ cutting into the meat _____ kill. Ancient man did _____ have the sharp teeth _____ a wolf or a _____ or a dog has. _____ _____ Man had seen fire _____ times. Along with the _____ animals, he had run _____ it. He too was _____ of fire.

Many brush _____ and grass fires were _____ by lightning, as they _____ are today.

Lightning hits _____ bush or a field _____ dry grass, and soon _____ is a big fire. _____ of the animals are afraid that the hunting _____ forget to hunt. When _____ is a big fire _____ them, a rabbit can _____ next to a coyote _____ being afraid.

Cloze Exercise   Level V

In 1925, a small _____ was blasted from its _____ frame in a laboratory. _____ twenty-seven seconds it _____. It was the first _____-fueled rocket to fly. _____ rocket would soon be _____ for testing in longer _____.

The rocket's inventor, Dr. _____ Goddard, was a tall, _____ _____ college teacher. When he _____ spare time from his _____ he experimented in the _____. For Dr. Goddard had _____ dream of building a _____ powerful enough to reach _____ altitudes. He was sure _____ only a rocket would _____ that because it didn't _____ air to make it _____.

Cloze Exercise   Level VI

Germany has contributed much _____ western civilization, despite her _____ past. Composers include Bach, _____ Mozart, and Wagner. Artists _____ Dürer and Holbein. The _____ _____ poets and other writers _____ Goethe, Kafka, and Mann. _____ and von Braun are among _____ most famous of the _____ scientists.

The tourist industry ————————— important to the West ————
————————. Five million tourists arrive ————————— year to view West
————————— varied attractions. Many of ————————— cities have an old
————————— atmosphere. Visitors may take ————————— boat tour
down the ————————— Rhine River. Some people ————————— sporting
thrills like skiing ————————— the southern mountain resorts. —————————
who visit the "Land ————————— Industry" are almost certain —————————
————————— return.

CLOZE EXERCISES ANSWER SHEET

Level

I	II	III	IV	V	VI
said	a	animals	be	rocket	to
in	would	among	was	testing	warlike
around	work	have	learn	for	Beethoven
like	children	down	out	flew	include
then	keeper	called	used	liquid	many
out	but	breathe	the	the	include
was	hard	sides	man	ready	Einstein
its	them	are	larger	flight	the
big	keeper	scales	stick	Robert	world's
pet	animals	instead	and	thin	is
Bill	than	fish	not	found	Germans
milk	a	help	that	teaching	each
into	everyone	there	for	laboratory	Germany's
saw	in	of	they	the	the
get	animals	ocean	not	projectile	world
we	same	water	that	high	a
very	works	in	lion	that	beautiful
for	cages	salt	Ancient	do	enjoy
for	be	fish	many	need	in
and	haircuts	color	wild	fly	those
pet	cleaned	rivers	from		of
back	swept	water	afraid		to
it	a	called	fires		
looked	ask	are	started		
oh	want	gray	still		
get	lions	group	a		
run	what	called	of		
not	others	not	there		
skunk	to	to	all		
	boys	would	so		
	to	backbone	animals		
	fun	near	there		
	animals	are	behind		
		that	run		
			without		

SUMMARY

Silent reading is a basic skill. For many people it is the most important of the skills acquired in the school setting. The assessment of silent reading through both the conventional graded silent reading paragraphs and the cloze procedures should provide the teacher with considerable information on the child's ability to read and comprehend silently.

Silent Reading Check Sheet

STUDENTS	Silent Reading Level	Rate	Comprehensive Literal	Interpretive	Inferential	Cloze Reading Level													

EIGHT

Study and Reference Skills

Frequently the terms "learning to read" and "reading to learn" are found together in educational literature because of the realization that the two tasks are central to the learning process in our public school system. From the middle elementary grades through graduate school a major source of information is the printed word. Even in the midst of a technological society the most routine and mechanical tasks usually involve some response to words in print. Our dependence on reading is apparent in our daily living patterns. Often the reading we do requires us to utilize study and reference skills to gain information. Whether we study a map to find a friend's home, look up a business in the telephone book, or study a manual to assemble a child's Christmas toy, we need these essential skills. The ability to read and to retain what is read is vital to success in life as well as in school.

In the early and middle elementary years the establishment of habits that foster study and reference skills will greatly enhance the child's effectiveness in utilizing study time and the printed learning resources at his disposal. Among the basic processes related to learning and the study skills are:

1. Reading and study skills
   a. Reading for the general idea (or scanning)
   b. Reading for specific information
   c. Locating information
2. Word information skills

3. Literary appreciation and analysis

In the next section of this chapter we will analyze these skills and their usefulness in the reading repertoire of each child.

READING AND STUDY SKILLS

Scanning refers to the process of "reading" a large section of print for a particular purpose in a relatively short period of time while giving little attention to the irrelevant sections of the material. Reading for the general idea may be included in the term, and there are several other subskills we can consider here as well. Scanning may be used to find the general structure in reading material. The child can gather this information by rapidly reading in the headings and the lead sentences in each paragraph. This can be done a page or two at a time or for an entire chapter, depending on the purpose. When a book is the source from which information is being gathered, the preface together with the summaries of chapters and sections can provide a student with a general idea of the structure of the material and its level of detail.

The scanning process gives the student data on which he can base further decisions regarding his studying. For example, what portions of a book are particularly relevant to his needs? Such an approach presupposes that the student does have a purpose in his reading. Often the matter of purpose is one where the teacher should supply careful guidance. Children do not automatically establish a purpose for reading before they begin. While doing so is not a reading skill per se, it can make the reading process itself more efficient since the student has something to look for as he begins. If the teacher helps children choose purposes, especially when dealing with content material, she will also help them acquire a valuable habit.

The concept of scanning can also be utilized in locating specific information. This includes searching for key words that can identify the content the reader is seeking. He can also locate specific information in a more general way by finding the main ideas of the passage and rapidly rereading the relevant portions for this information. Such a process reduces the amount of material to be read and the amount of time necessary to accomplish a given task.

Describing these methods does not imply that all or even most reading for information should be of a narrow and specific nature. Certainly much that an author has to say about a subject cannot be predetermined and isolated, nor should it be. We mean that it is highly desirable to provide the student with a variety of skills for seeking information and using printed material so that in the course of his study he can best utilize the resources at his command. An able and flexible reader can use such procedures with great speed and efficiency.

Another subskill in this area involves the reader's organizing his own concept of the material he is reading. A reader has the choice of either following the author's organization and thought or superimposing his own organizational pattern on the material. Oddly enough, it rarely occurs to children that it is possible to read a book in any other order than the author's. Teachers need to help children become aware of the varied possibilities open to them. Discussing and choosing a purpose for reading and scaning for general format and key ideas can help the reader make this kind of judgment.

Analysis of an author's sources is another study skill that can be most helpful to the student. This implies use of resources in a book such as the bibliography, footnotes, and quotations. When conflicts appear once or twice among sources, such factors as date of publication and the author's background and potential biases can be analyzed. This may require the student to go beyond his present material and venture toward independent research. If study and reference skills are considered a part of the reading area, it is easy to see the value of the learning experiences that result from inquiring into the nature of the circumstances surrounding the author and his point of view at the time he wrote. All these skills can be developed through the scanning technique or can be explored in greater depth depending on the needs and maturity of the class.

This approach to reading material frequently requires skills in using reference works, textbooks, and the like that go beyond the reading process itself. Critical thinking and evaluation are inherent in this approach. The use of such information location tools as the table of contents, chapter headings, and the index of a book can prove to be vital when reading for information.

The skills associated with these portions of a book include alphabetizing, scanning for key words, and the use of guide words and headings of all kinds. Frequently overlooked in this process is the skill of categorizing and identifying synonyms. In using an index, for example, it is often necessary to search for a general category in which specific information can be found rather than for a certain word. The use of synonyms and alternate forms of a word or the reduction of a phrase to its most important words is of great value in this process. If a student is seeking information on the Wright brothers' first flight, what word would he look for in the index? Perhaps words that don't even appear in the statement would be most useful. In this example such words as "airplane" or "aviation" would probably be the key to the information sought.

Particularly in areas of study that require multiple sources of information for problem-solving purposes, the use of the table of contents and the index must be automatic. An acquaintance with these reference tools should begin in the primary years for most children. The teacher can build the utilization of these tools into early reading experiences and make it habitual. By the middle years the differences between the table of contents and the index and the association of these two guides to the contents of the work should be clearly in the mind of the child. The use of such books as an encyclopedia starts in the middle elementary years and continues to grow through secondary school. The use of reference indexes such as the *Readers' Guide to Periodical Literature* and the library's card catalog necessarily involves extension of the skills acquired in the child's first reading experiences.

In approaching resource materials, the ability to scan can be critical. Rapid reading of the lists in the index or table of contents avoids wasting time and can even help avoid "distracting" alternatives. We probably do more scanning in these kinds of lists (from the telephone book to the mail order catalog) than any other single resource.

WORD INFORMATION SKILLS

The use of a dictionary to obtain word information can begin early in a child's reading experiences. Close acquaintance with this resource can become a central part of learning study skills. The efficient and proper use of dictionaries is a basic necessity if "reading to learn" is to become a part of the repertoire of a student. Encounters with new or unfamiliar words will be a regular occurrence and can be a positive and challenging experience even for the less able reader. But the experience must be closely related to both the needs of the child and the child's ability. When reference to dictionaries is a regular and consistent part of classroom activity, the children will probably master the necessary skills more easily.

The earliest skill utilized will be alphabetization. This leads quickly to the use of guide words and can usually be learned in the early grades. In the middle and upper grades children should be able to demonstrate skill with the phonetic keys in a dictionary. The diacritical markings and the accent marks give a reader much useful information and need to be specifically taught. The use of the definitions themselves, together with synonyms and antonyms, constitutes the heart of the information contained in any dictionary.

The thesaurus, like the dictionary, can be a useful tool in both the reading and writing of words, but it usually comes into use later than the regular dictionary. Syno-

nyms, antonyms, and the shades of meaning that go beyond the literal can be found here. Again, information location skills such as the use of guide words and alphabetizing are very important in the efficient use of this reference work.

LITERARY APPRECIATION AND ANALYSIS

Information-finding methods should carry over from one task to another. Though the goals of a lesson in literary appreciation may be very different from a content-oriented social studies lesson, many of the techniques of information location such as alphabetizing, scanning, reading for specific information, and the use of chapter headings and the like can be valuable. We can ask questions concerning the author's purpose and our own purpose in reading the material. We can scan to see if the material is compatible with our goals. (Some people have been known to even scan the ending—just in case!) We can research information about the author from other sources or, if we like his material, other books or stories he may have written. If we are stressing "reading to learn," then our basic study skills will be useful regardless of the particular material we are reading.

SCANNING TEST

The test for scanning is constructed in two parts. Part A consists of scanning a particular passage for specific words or phrases. The child counts the number of times the word or phrase appears in the passage and records it on his answer sheet. Each section has a time limit to encourage rapid reading. All passages are selected from content areas, and words or phrases to be found are related to key issues in the material. A check question is included with each paragraph.

The second part of the test identifies skills in locating general ideas in a passage. The teacher times the reading, and then the student must identify the main concept or best title for the passage and decide whether it would provide information about a particular topic. A multiple-choice format may be used in Part B of the test for ease of correction.

Part A

Directions to the teacher:

In this test each child will need copies of the sample paragraph and the five testing paragraphs on separate sheets. Children's paragraphs should not list the important words, ideas, or check questions. Each child will also need an answer sheet. All sheets should be passed out in advance and kept face down on the desk until they are needed. If the last paragraph, E, is passed out first, then D, and so on, they will be in the correct order. The reading of each paragraph is timed, so the use of a watch with a sweep second hand or a stop watch is advisable. Give the directions clearly and check the answers to the sample paragraph to make sure everyone understands. Do not allow the children to look back at the paragraph after time is called.

Directions to the children:

Read each paragraph to follow silently in the time limit I give you. As you read it, remember the number of times you see the "important" word or phrase. Read as quickly as you can without missing the word you are looking for or the important idea of the story. Then I will tell you to turn the page over. When I ask you to, you will write the number of times you found the "important" word or idea on the answer sheet beside the question number. Then I will read the check questions to you and you will mark the correct space on the answer sheet.

Now let's try one. (Distribute sample sheet face down.) This sheet should be kept face down until I tell you to turn it over. The important word is "mother." Remember the number of times you find "mother" in the sample paragraph. You will have ten seconds to read this paragraph. When I say begin, turn the sheet over and start reading silently, remembering the number of times you see "mother." When I say "stop," turn the sheet face down and listen for further directions. Are there any questions? Ready? Begin.

After ten seconds, say: Stop! Turn your sheet face down. Look at your answer sheet. Beside the S-1 write the number of times you saw the word "mother" in the sample paragraph. Now for the check question. Beside the S-2, write the color of the moth that fluttered to a landing. . . . How many of you wrote the number three and wrote the word "brown"? Good! The word "mother" appeared three times in the paragraph, and the paragraph said the moth was brown. Turn the sheet over and reread the sample to check your answer.

Now turn over sheet A. The important word is "sail." Remember the number of times you find "sail" in the paragraph. You will have ten seconds to read this paragraph. When I say begin, turn the sheet over and start reading silently. Begin! (Ten seconds later:) Stop! Turn the sheet over. Beside the A-1 on your answer sheet, write the number of times you saw the word "sail." Now for the check question. Beside the A-2, write the place Christopher wanted to sail to.

Now turn over sheet B. The important word is "made." Remember the number of times you find "made" in the paragraph. You will have ten seconds to read this paragraph. When I say "begin," turn the card over and start reading silently. Begin! (Ten seconds later:) Stop! Turn the paper over. Beside the B-1 on the answer sheet, write the number of times you saw the word "made." Beside the B-2, write the thing that brick is made of. (For C-E only.) If a question calls for a yes or no answer, circle the "yes" or "no" on the answer sheet.

Now turn over sheet C. (Repeat directions as above, using the important phrases or words listed below. Note the check questions as indicated. Repeat the above for sheets D and E.)

Paragraph C

Reading time: Fifteen seconds.
Important word: Philosopher.
Important ideas: (C-2) Does the paragraph tell how the atom was first named?
                   (C-3) Does the paragraph tell how Democritus proved his idea?
Check Question: (C-4) How long ago did Democritus live?

Paragraph D

Reading time: Twenty seconds.
Important word: Engineering.
Important ideas: (D-2) Does the drill-and-blast method require few men?
                   (D-3) Does the paragraph tell how long it took to dig the tunnel?
                   (D-4) Does the paragraph tell how the tunnel was to be used?
Check question: (D-5) How long was the tunnel?

Paragraph E

Reading time: Twenty seconds.
Important word: Carton.
Important ideas: (E-2) Does the paragraph tell how to make a stage?
                   (E-3) Does the paragraph tell how wide the frame should be?
                   (E-4) Does the paragraph tell how to make a curtain?
Check question: (E-5) Which part should you cut off?

Sample Paragraph

Possum was warm and snug, riding in the pouch under his mother. But he couldn't see anything in there. Pushing his head through the opening, he peered at the outside world. His mother was up in a tree! Then she saw a big brown moth flutter to a landing. The mother possum snapped it up.

Paragraph A

When Christopher was older, he could sail the little boat himself. "I like to sail a boat," he said. "I would like to learn to be a sailor." "You must learn to be a weaver," his father said. Christopher learned to clean wool and to make the wool into cloth. But more than anything else, he wanted to sail. His dream was to sail to a place called India that he had never seen.

Paragraph B

Have you ever wondered what all the things you see around you are made of? A house may be made of brick, and if you look closely, you can see that the brick is made up of little lumps of hard clay. Each little lump is made up of still smaller ones. How little do you suppose the littlest one is?

Paragraph C

The ancient Greeks liked to talk and argue about all kinds of things. The people who would argue the most were called philosophers. One philosopher thought that if he cut up things into smaller and smaller pieces he would come to pieces that couldn't be cut down any further. These pieces he called atoms. This philosopher was called Democritus. He lived 2500 years ago. He was considered the father of the atom.

Paragraph D

When the men came to high and rugged mountains, they wondered how they were going to get to the other side. The engineering problems that they faced were very difficult. The mountains were made of hard granite rock and the mountains themselves were very high. The decision was made to dig a tunnel through the mountains. It would have to be almost ¼ mile long and much of it would have to be drill-and-blast digging through the granite bed rock. This situation called for a large number of workers who would be willing to do very heavy work for long periods of time.

Paragraph E

A cardboard carton makes a good puppet stage. Cut off the top of the carton. Don't cut the sides or the bottom. Trim the sides of the carton to about 14 inches. Cut out the center part of the bottom of the carton in a square. Leave a frame five inches wide. Now put the carton on the table standing on one side and you have a puppet stage.

TEACHER'S ANSWER SHEET

Sample Paragraph

S-1	3
S-2	brown

Paragraph A

A-1	4
A-2	India

Paragraph B

B-1	4
B-2	hard clay

Paragraph C

C-1	2
C-2	no
C-3	no
C-4	2500 years

Paragraph D

D-1　1 _____
D-2　no _____
D-3　no _____
D-4　no _____
D-5　¼ mile _____

Paragraph E

E-1　5 _____
E-2　yes _____
E-3　yes _____
E-4　no _____
E-5　top _____

TEST FOR SCANNING FOR INFORMATION　　LEVEL I
STUDENT ANSWER SHEET

Name _____

Sample Paragraph

S-1　_____
S-2　_____

Paragraph A

A-1　_____
A-2　_____

Paragraph B

B-1　_____
B-2　_____

Paragraph C

C-1　_____
C-2　yes　no
C-3　yes　no
C-4　_____

Paragraph D

D-1　_____
D-2　yes　no
D-3　yes　no
D-4　yes　no
D-5　_____

Paragraph E

E-1 _____

E-2   yes   no

E-3   yes   no

E-4   yes   no

E-5 _____

TEST FOR SCANNING FOR INFORMATION

Part B

Directions to the teacher:

In this test you are to ask the child to determine the general idea of a passage by scanning it and then to determine if it is related to a prestated study topic. As in part *A*, all test readings are timed to ensure that scanning is being done. This is not designed as a reading comprehension test per se, though it may be used as such if it suits the purposes of the teacher. The child will need a copy of each paragraph on separate sheets and a blank paper on which to write his answers. State the topic for study *before* the time to begin reading is called. Be sure to check the answers on the sample.

Directions to the children:

Read each paragraph as directed. Be careful to read rapidly because the time you have will be short. Then on your blank paper write the letter of the paragraph and the number of the title of the passage that I read. Choose the title that you think best fits the paragraph. Then I will ask you whether the paragraph you have read will help you to learn more about the subject for study. Write "yes" or "no" to show if it will help or not. Let's try one.

Sample Paragraph

Topic for study: The history of flight.
Reading time: Thirty seconds.
Which title is the best for this passage?

    1.   Flying Past and Present
    2.   Space Flight and Today's Planes
    3.   The Jet in War and Peace
    4.   Improving Our Airports

Does this paragraph fit the topic of study? No, there is no relation to history, the key concept in the topic. Let's check. You should have written "*S*" for the paragraph. Then 2 for the best title. After the number 2 you should have the word "no." (Write on the board if necessary: S-2, no.)

Paragraph A

Topic for study: Modern health problems in underdeveloped countries.
Reading time: Thirty seconds.
Best title for this paragraph:

1. Life in a Poor Country
2. Industrial Pollution
3. The Care of Babies
4. How to Grow Crops for Your Family

(Answer: 1)

Does the paragraph fit the topic of study?   (Yes)

Paragraph B

Topic for study: Space in the atomic age.
Reading time: Twenty seconds.
Best title for this paragraph:

1. Matter Is Made of Empty Space
2. The Relationship of the Atom
3. Picturing the Size of the Atom
4. Enlarging the Atom

(Answer: 3)

Does the paragraph fit the topic of study?   (No)

Paragraph S

On a bright day in June, the large Boeing 747 lifted off the runway at the airport. There were over 300 passengers and crew aboard. It is seldom that the passengers in these flights are disturbed by the fact that they are flying at incredibly high altitudes or that their very lives depend on thousands of mechanical parts working exactly as they should. The future of flight, particularly space flight, is even more difficult to understand; yet it is coming, and the time is not too far in the future when we will think it as commonplace as the modern jet ride of today.

Paragraph A

Many of the industrialized countries of the world have problems that are difficult for their leaders to solve. But in the countries that have little or no knowledge of the modern factory or farm, the problems of the survival of the people themselves is almost beyond the imagination. For example, in some countries, where the climate is not ideal for living, there is one baby who dies for every two babies born. The problems of feeding and clothing the people in some countries even with the simplest kinds of goods is beyond the means available, and the result is starvation and death by disease of large numbers of the people. The people who do survive are so busy just providing for themselves and their families that they have little time and energy to help their countries solve the large problems that they face.

Paragraph B

Can we get an idea of the size of the atom and its nucleus? If we could make the whole atom a million times bigger it would be about as big as a pinhead. If we wanted to see the nucleus, we would have to enlarge the atom twenty thousand million times. The atom would be as big as a large trailer but we would just barely be able to see the nucleus itself. Mostly we would see vast empty spaces between the nucleus and its electrons because the greatest part of all matter is empty space.

WORD INFORMATION TESTS

This section involves a number of different tests for specific skills.

Alphabetizing Skills Test

Alphabetizing skills are tested through the location and insertion of words in an alphabetical list at level I and the writing of words in alphabetical order at level II. At level III, the use of guide words is tested by giving the children sample guide words with page numbers as they would appear in a dictionary. A list of words must be matched to the correct page numbers that the guide words would indicate.

ALPHABETIZING SKILLS TEST   LEVEL I

Directions to the teacher:

This test has two parts. Each child will need an answer sheet. Give directions orally and check to make sure the first item in each part is done correctly.

Directions to the children:

Today we're going to see how well you can find words that are in alphabetical order. There are two parts to this job. First you will have to find some words in an alphabetical list and put the correct number beside the word you were looking for. Look at your paper. The list at the top is in alphabetical order. Now look at part A. The first word is "doll." What is the number of the word "doll"? You will do the rest in a moment.

In part B the words are not in the alphabetical list and you must figure out where they would belong. Look at part B. It says, "The next words are not on the list. Where should they go?" The first word is "me." Look at the list. Between what two words would "me" fit? (Give the children an opportunity to find the answer.) Yes, the word "me" would go between "man" and "mother" because "man" has an "m" and then an "a" while "mother" has an "m" and then an "o." The word "me" has an "m" and then an "e" and "e" is between "a" and "o" in the alphabet. What are the numbers of "man" and "mother"? Right. So we will write 15 and 16 on our answer sheet and then it will read "me: between 15 and 16." Are there any questions? (Do on the board if necessary.) You may begin now. Do part A first and then part B.

ALPHABETIZING TEST

Alphabetical List

1.	apple	13.	is
2.	are	14.	like
3.	baby	15.	man
4.	birthday	16.	mother
5.	come	17.	name
6.	doll	18.	play
7.	eat	19.	put
8.	girl	20.	run
9.	go	21.	saw
10.	has	22.	that
11.	here	23.	them
12.	house	24.	want

Part A   What number is the word?

doll ⸻ *(6)*   that ⸻ *(22)*
go ⸻ *(9)*   is ⸻ *(13)*
like ⸻ *(14)*   here ⸻ *(11)*
run ⸻ *(20)*   come ⸻ *(5)*
are ⸻ *(2)*   mother ⸻ *(16)*

ALPHABETIZING TEST

Part B   The next words are not on the list. Where should they go?

me: between ⸻ and ⸻ *(15–16)*
pretty: between ⸻ and ⸻ *(18–19)*
be: between ⸻ and ⸻ *(3–4)*
one: between ⸻ and ⸻ *(17–18)*
the: between ⸻ and ⸻ *(22–23)*
his: between ⸻ and ⸻ *(11–12)*
up: between ⸻ and ⸻ *(23–24)*
just: between ⸻ and ⸻ *(13–14)*
did: between ⸻ and ⸻ *(5–6)*
school: between ⸻ and ⸻ *(21–22)*

ALPHABETIZING TEST

Name ⸻

Alphabetical List

1. apple
2. are
3. baby
4. birthday
5. come
6. doll
7. eat
8. girl
9. go
10. has
11. here
12. house

13. is
14. like
15. man
16. mother
17. name
18. play
19. put
20. run
21. saw
22. that
23. them
24. want

Part A   What number is the word?

doll ⸻   that ⸻
go ⸻   is ⸻
like ⸻   here ⸻
run ⸻   come ⸻
are ⸻   mother ⸻

Name _____

Part B   The next words are not on the list.
Where should they go?

me: between _____ and _____

pretty: between _____ and _____

be: between _____ and _____

one: between _____ and _____

the: between _____ and _____

his: between _____ and _____

up: between _____ and _____

just: between _____ and _____

did: between _____ and _____

school: between _____ and _____

ALPHABETIZING SKILLS TEST   *LEVEL II*

Directions to the teacher:

Each child will need a sheet with the groups of words to be alphabetized. He can rewrite these words in the correct order or put numbers next to them to indicate the correct alphabetical order. The second approach is more difficult but may help the child who has handwriting difficulties. Do the sample group with the children and check to make sure they have done it correctly.

Directions to the children:

On the paper that we have just passed out you will see that there are six boxes. In each box there is a group of words that you are to put in alphabetical order. You are to (teacher chooses):

(1) Write the words again in the box in the correct order.

(2) Put numbers next to the words showing the alphabetical order—a 1 beside the word that would come first, a 2 beside the one that would come next, and so on.

We will do the sample together. Which word should come first? (Do the sample with the group.) Now do the rest of the boxes by yourself.

SAMPLE	A
home	big
ball	think
please	because
water	after
some	pull

B	C
head	blown
hand	bleat
hug	blue
hope	blowing
high	bluster
	black
	blustery

D	E
mental	thermoelectric
menial	thermos
menu	thermograph
menthol	thermal
mentality	thermonuclear
mend	thermidor
menace	thermostat
menagerie	thermotherapy
	thermionics
	thermometry

ALPHABETIZING SKILLS TEST   LEVEL III

Directions to the teacher:

This test has two parts. The first part requires the child to decide whether certain words would be on a sample page by using the guide words. In the second part he must decide on what page a particular word would be. Each child will need an answer sheet. You may want to put part A and part B on separate sheets so that you can give half of the test at one sitting. Read the top section of the student page to the group and answer any questions about guide words before beginning. Do the sample with the class and check to make sure everyone understands part A. In part B, you may do the first answer with the group.

Directions to the children:

Today we are going to do some work using guide words. Listen while I read the section from the top of the page. (Read to the group and answer any questions.) Now let's do the sample. (Do with the group.)

In part *B* the only difference is that you must decide which of these file pages the words would go on, and write the page number after the word. What page would the word "instrument" go on? Yes, page 615; write it. Do parts *A* and *B*.

ALPHABETIZING SKILLS TEST   LEVEL III

Guide words are found at the top of each page in the dictionary and in some other reference books. They are repeating the first word on the page and the last word on the page. They can help us find words more quickly. They look like this:

Sample:

baby	89	ball

Circle the words that would be on this page:

baffle   back   break   baa   banner

Part A

1.
trump	950	trust

trumpet   trunk   tree   truss   truly

2.
veterinarian	1258	vicar

vexed   vestry   vial   vibrate   victory

3.
fortune	325	foul

fortunate   fossil   forward   foster   found

4.
blind	98	blood

block   blend   bleed   bliss   blot

5.
untold	1303	up

unto   untrue   untangle   untouchable   unwritten

ALPHABETIZING SKILLS TEST   LEVEL III

Name _____

Part B

instantaneously	615	insufficient
insufficiently	616	integrator
integrity	617	intensive
knavery	652	knock
knockabout	653	k.o.

The following word would be on what page?

Sample: intense   <u>617</u>

1.	instrument _____	(615)
2.	knob _____	(652)
3.	intact _____	(616)
4.	integral _____	(616)
5.	instinct _____	(615)
6.	knuckle _____	(653)
7.	insurance _____	(616)
8.	knell _____	(652)
9.	insufficiency _____	(615)
10.	intelligence _____	(617)
11.	knot _____	(653)
12.	intended _____	(617)

ALPHABETIZING SKILLS TEST
ANSWER SHEET

Part A

Sample   baffle, back

1. trumpet, trunk, truss, truly
2. vexed, vial, vibrate
3. fossil, forward, foster
4. block, bliss
5. untrue, untouchable, unwritten

Part B

Sample   617

1.	615		7.	616
2.	652		8.	652
3.	616		9.	615
4.	616		10.	617
5.	615		11.	653
6.	653		12.	617

Phonetic Dictionary Skills Test

Phonetic keys, diacritical markings, and accents are used in the next test. The keys and accent patterns are provided on a separate sheet. At one level the child will be asked to match a known word to its phonetic spelling, such as "cat" to "kat" or "does" to "duz." At the next level he must write the word from a phonetic spelling. For example, the word "sez" is really spelled "says." For diacritical markings he will choose between two possible answers to a question.

Example: which do you wear on your foot?

sho̅   shü

In the test for use of accent markings the child must choose between words that are spelled the same but accented differently.

Example: The escaped _____ was frightened.

con'vict   con víct

Note:

A separate sample pronunciation key is included that is similar to those found at the beginning of any dictionary. It is meant to be used with the first three levels of this test. Since all dictionaries vary slightly in the markings they use, do *not* use your regular classroom dictionaries for these activities.

LEVEL I

Directions to the teacher:

Each child will need a test and a sample pronunciation key. Do the sample with the children to make sure they all understand. The first part of the directions to the children can be used for any of the levels.

Directions to the children:

As you know, letters in English can have more than one sound. When you go to look a word up in the dictionary you often find the word spelled differently in parentheses after the real spelling. That is to help you pronounce a new word. The different symbols for this kind of spelling are always found in a pronunciation key at the beginning of the dictionary. Today you are going to get a sample pronunciation key like one you would find in the dictionary and we will see if you can use it. Everyone look at the "key" for a moment. . . . Now let's look at your work sheet. (The first part of the directions to the children can be used for any of the levels.)

    On one edge of the paper are the special phonetic spellings and on the other are the regular spellings. You are going to try matching the two kinds of spellings. At the top of the page is a sample; let's do that together. What word matches the phonetic spelling "k-a-t" (spell out)? Right—"cat." What number should you put after the phonetic spelling, then? "Three" is correct. What about the next one? (Do samples with the group.) Now do the rest of the page on your own. If you are not sure, use your sample pronunciation key to help you.

SAMPLE PRONUNCIATION KEY

Accent Markings:

(/), as in mother (muth′ ər), is used to mark primary accent or stress; the syllable preceding it is pronounced with greater emphasis than other syllables in the word. Silent letters are not included. Upside-down letters stand for unaccented syllables: ə ; ℇ in alone, ə in system.

ă	act, mat	ŏ	clock, hot
ā	able, cake	ō	own, no
ã	dare, chair	ô	corn, call
ä	car, calm	oi	oil, boy

b	back, tub	ou	cloud, out
ch	choose, beach	p	pat, top
d	do, Ted	r	rake, cry
ĕ	shell, set	s	saw, hiss
ē	knee, equal	sh	shoe, push
f	fit, farmer	t	ten, pit
g	beg, get	th	thin, path
h	hit, hat	ŧh	then, breathe
hw	when, why	ŭ	sun, love
ĭ	chill, if	ū	cute, few
ī	rise, flight	ũ	urge, bird
j	just, edge	u̇	pull, took
k	kept, cap	ü	true, ooze
l	low, all	v	voice, live
m	mine, Tim	w	west, way
n	on, now	y	you, yes
		z	zeal, those
		zh	vision, beige

PHONETIC DICTIONARY SKILLS TEST   LEVEL I

Name ————————————

Sample:

kăt ————————

sĕl ————————

rĕk ————————

1. cell
2. wreck
3. cat

---

lŭnj ————————

kŭp ————————

kwĭp ————————

thrĕd ————————

gĕst ————————

dŭz ————————

prĭns ————————

krŭm ————————

mĭks ————————

tŭng ————————

jĕm ————————

boi ————————

glü ————————

dŏut ————————

ku̇d ————————

1. gem
2. tongue
3. cup
4. glue
5. lunge
6. thread
7. mix
8. boy
9. quip
10. crumb
11. could
12. guest
13. does
14. doubt
15. prince

lunj	5
kup	3
kwip	9
thred	6
guest	12
duz	13
prins	15
krum	10
miks	7
tung	2
jem	1
boi	8
glu	4
dout	14
kud	11

PHONETIC DICTIONARY SKILLS TEST   LEVEL II

Directions to the teacher:

The children will each need a sample pronunciation key and a test sheet. If they have not done level I or if it has been some time since they did, you may want to use the initial section of those directions concerning the key.

Directions to the children:

(Repeat any of the previous directions necessary.) Today you are going to try to figure out the real spelling for a word that is in the special phonetic spelling. You will probably need to refer to your sample pronunciation key to find out what the word should be. Then you will write the correct spelling next to the special one. First there are two samples to try at the top of the page. Let's do them now. Who can pronounce the word? How would you spell it? If you are not sure, look under "z" in your pronunciation key. What are two ways to spell that sound? Write says "s-a-y-s" after the sample *A*. (Repeat for *B*.) Now try numbers 1 to 10 by yourself.

PHONETIC DICTIONARY SKILLS TEST   LEVEL II

Name _____

Sample:

    a. sĕz _____   (says)
    b. klŏk _____   (clock)

---

    1. fĕns _____   (fence)
    2. kŭm _____   (come)

3.	flŭd	————————	(flood)
4.	lăm	————————	(lamb)
5.	rüm	————————	(room)
6.	noiz	————————	(noise)
7.	kôf	————————	(cough)
8.	lăf	————————	(laugh)
9.	bu̇k	————————	(book)
10.	bāzh	————————	(beige)

PHONETIC DICTIONARY SKILLS TEST   LEVEL III

Directions to the teacher:

The children will need a sample pronunciation key and a test sheet. The initial directions regarding the key may be used as desired. Complete the samples with the group and check the answers.

Directions to the children:

In the work we are going to do today you will read a sentence and then decide which of the two phonetic spellings represent the word that is underlined in the sentence. You can use your sample pronunciation key to help you. Both the sounds and the accent marks will help you. Circle the spelling that correctly represents the underlined word. Let's try sample A. Who can read the sentence? . . . Which of the two spellings represents the underlined word? Right! The first word would be pronounced "quite" and it's one syllable. The second is two syllables and is pronounced "quiet." Complete Sample B by yourself and then we'll check it together. . . . What is the correct answer to sample B? Good. Are there any questions?

PHONETIC DICTIONARY SKILLS TEST   LEVEL III

Name ————————————

Directions:

Circle the phonetic spelling that stands for the underlined word.

Sample A

The night was very <u>quiet</u>.
    a. kwĭt   b. kwī' et

Sample B

You are very <u>definite</u> about the answer.
    a. dĕf' e nĭt   b. dĭ fī' nt

(b)   1.   Whose dog is that?

                 a.   hōz   b.   hüz

(b)   2.   A whale is a huge sea animal.

                 a.   hălb   b.   hwāl

(b)   3.   I would like to be an ice skater.

                 a.   skăt r'   b.   skāt' r

(a)   4.   The blue bird is very pretty.

                 a.   bũrd   b.   brīd

(a)   5.   Pour the water from the pitcher.

                 a.   pĭch' r   b.   pĭk'ch r

(a)   6.   The author wrote many good books.

                 a.   ô'ther   b.   ŭth'er

(b)   7.   He has one black shoe and one brown one.

                 a.   shō   b.   shü

(b)   8.   Please cancel the order.

                 a.   kăn sel'   b.   kăn's l

(a)   9.   His job is below hers.

                 a.   bi lō'   b.   bĕl'ō

(b)   10.   Who is the main character?

                 a.   chăr' ti   b.   kăr'ĭk tr

PHONETIC DICTIONARY SKILLS TEST   LEVEL IV

Directions to the teacher:

A test sheet will be needed. The sample pronunciation key is optional, since only the information on accent will be relevant to this test. Complete the samples with the group to make sure they understand the concept.

Directions to the children:

On the worksheet you have today you can see some sentences with a word missing in each one. Below each sentence are two words; they look alike, but they are pronounced differently. The accent mark tells you which part of the word is stressed more, and that information tells you which word is correct for the sentence. You will circle the correct one. Let's work Sample A together. Read the sentence, please. . . . Now look at the two words. How would you say the first word? . . . How would you say the second word? . . . Which one is correct for the sentence? Read it, please. Everyone circle the correct word. Now try Sample B on your own. . . . Which word is correct? Read the sentence. Good! You can begin now.

Name _____

Sample A

The escaped _____ was frightened.

(a)   a. con'vict   b. con vict'

Sample B

I know nothing about the _____.

(a)   a. sub'ject   b. sub ject'

_____

(a)   1. We made good _____ in arithmetic.
            a. prog'ress   b. pro gress'

(a)   2. The men were lost in the _____.
            a. dez'ert   b. de zurt'

(b)   3. I bought a new _____ today.
            a. re kord'   b. rek'ərd

(a)   4. There was a large pile of _____ by the curb.
            a. ref'us   b. re fuz'

(a)   5. I received a watch for a _____.
            a. pres'ent   b. pre sent'

(a)   6. He got a _____ to sell candy.
            a. per'mit   b. per mit'

(a)   7. You must give me a _____.
            a. re'fund   b. re fund'

(b)   8. Many _____ fought against the government.
            a. re bels'   b. re'bels

(b)   9. I am _____ to stay here.
            a. kon'tent   b. kon tent'

(b)   10. Will you _____ me home?
            a. kon'duct   b. kən duct'

Dictionary Definitions Test

The last test in this section concerns the selection of a word through its definition. Definitions of words with multiple meanings are provided, and the child must use the definition that would be appropriate in a particular sentence.

DICTIONARY DEFINITIONS TEST

Directions to the teacher:

The children will need a copy of the test. A separate answer sheet may be used if desired. A sample is provided for work with the class.

Directions to the children:

Many times when we don't know what a word means we go to the dictionary to find out. Sometimes when we do that, we find more than one meaning for a word and we have to figure out which meaning fits into the sentence we are reading. Today we are going to work on a paper to see how well you can figure out which meaning of a word should go into a particular sentence. Look at the sample on your paper. Who can read the definitions for the word "crane"? . . . Now read sentence A. Which of the four meanings for "crane" fits in this sentence? Right, d does; put a d (*either* on the line in front of the A *or* on your answer sheet after the letter A). How about sentence B? Yes small b is correct. Do the rest of the definitions in the same way. You may begin now.

DICTIONARY DEFINITIONS TEST

Name _____

Sample:

crane
  a. bird.
  b. machine for raising and lowering heavy weights.
  c. Any arm which swings about a vertical axis.
  d. stretch (the neck) as a crane does; [hence, to hesitate.]
(d) _____ A. I had to crane to see over the fence.
(b) _____ B. The arm of the crane lifted the automobile.

═══════════════════════════════

junk
  a. A particular type of boat found in the Far East.
  b. Old iron, glass, paper, etc. which may be used again in some form.
(b) _____ 1. He took a truckload of objects to the junk yard.
(a) _____ 2. The Chinese family lived on a junk.

═══════════════════════════════

row
  a. A noisy or turbulent quarrel.
  b. To propel with oars along the surface of the water.
(b) _____ 3. I can row the boat quickly.
(a) _____ 4. My neighbors had a real row last night.

═══════════════════════════════

cape
  a. A sleeveless garment fastened around the neck and falling loosely over the shoulders.
  b. A piece of land jutting into the sea.
(a) _____ 5. I loved my new blue cape.
(b) _____ 6. The cape was very rugged.

═══════════════════════════════

flicker
  a. To burn unsteadily.
  b. To wave to and fro.

      c. A brief spark.
      d. A North American woodpecker.

(c) ———— 7. He felt a small flicker of hope.
(d) ———— 8. The flicker made loud raucous noises.

═══════════════════════════════

flight
      a. Act, manner, or power of flying.
      b. The distance covered by a flying object.
      c. A number of beings flying.
      d. A journey by air.
      e. The series of steps or stairs between two adjacent landings.

(d) ———— 9. Our flight has been canceled.
(a) ———— 10. The discovery of flight was man's greatest invention.

═══════════════════════════════

fret
      a. An irritated state of mind.
      b. To cause corrosion; gnaw.
      c. Become eaten, worn, or corroded.
      d. An interlaced, angular design.
      e. Any of the ridges of wood, metal, or string set across the finger board of a lute or similar instrument.

(a) ———— 11. She will constantly fret about her money problems.
(d) ———— 12. The fretwork on the old church was beautiful.

═══════════════════════════════

lock
      a. A device for securing a door, gate, or lid.
      b. A device to keep a wheel from rotating.
      c. The mechanism in a firearm.
      d. An enclosed portion of a canal, river, etc., with gates at each end.
      e. Any of various grapples or holds in wrestling.
      f. To fasten or secure.
      g. To exclude.
      h. A tress or portion of hair.

(e) ———— 13. He had a hammer lock on his opponent.
(g) ———— 14. The business had a lock out against the strikers.
(c) ———— 15. The lock on the gun was broken.

INFORMATION LOCATION TESTS

Tests in this section are related to finding information in various typical resources such as a table of contents or indexes of various kinds. Level I, part A, consists of finding particular titles in a sample table of contents and listing the beginning pages. In part B the child must decide which chapter titles in the sample might contain information concerning a stated topic. Example: Which chapter might contain information about anteaters?

At level II, a sample index is given and the child must list all the sections that might contain information concerning his topic, first with page numbers, then with subject titles. At this level the ability to use synonyms will affect his performance. Will he look under aviation and aeronautics and early flights in space?

Level III tests the child's knowledge of other available resources. A list of various possible references such as the thesaurus and encyclopedia is given, and the children must choose which resources would contain particular information.

INFORMATION LOCATION TEST   LEVEL I

Directions to the teacher:

This test contains two parts. For each part the student will need the sample table of contents and a test sheet. Answers may be written on a separate answer sheet if desired. Work the sample with the class and check the answers. If a child has an answer not listed but can show you the reasoning that led to his choice, the answer should be accepted.

Directions to the children:

The table of contents is a very useful part of a book. I know you have all used it often. Today we have a sample table of contents and a work sheet with two parts to it. What is the book about that we have the table of contents for? The first part asks us to find the beginning page of the chapter that probably has information about a particular thing. Look at the sample in part *A*. What chapter might be about animals of the Indians? Right. What page does that chapter start on? Write the page number in the blank. (Check.) Now look at part *B*. Here we have a subject that might be in several chapters. We have to decide which ones might have the information we want. What subject is listed under sample *B*? Which chapter or chapters might have this information? (Answer: 7 and 14.) Put the number of the chapter on the line. Are there any questions? Remember, there can be several chapters that will fit. List all that might be right. Do part *A*, then part *B*. You may begin now.

SAMPLE TABLE OF CONTENTS

Chapter	Title	Page
1	Indians of Prehistory	8
2	Indian Horses	16
3	Sign Language and Picture Writing	23
4	Indian Sports and Pleasures	29
5	Indian Art	36
6	How an Indian Brave Lived	42
7	How an Indian Woman Lived	50
8	How the Medicine Men Lived	56
9	White Men Come to America	65
10	Early Treaties	75
11	Indian Massacres	85
12	On the Warpath	96
13	Custer's Last Stand	105
14	Indians Today	112
	Index	125

INFORMATION LOCATION TEST

Name _____

Part A

Write the page number for the chapter that probably tells you about the following things.

Sample A		Animals of the Indians	(16) _____
(56)	1.	Indian medicine	_____
(105)	2.	A famous battle	_____
(8)	3.	The earliest Indians	_____
(36)	4.	Pictures by Indians	_____
(75)	5.	Agreements signed with Indians	_____
(112)	6.	How Indians live now	_____
(29)	7.	Games Indians played	_____
(50)	8.	Jobs of an Indian woman	_____
(23)	9.	Ways Indians wrote things down	_____
(42)	10.	How a brave caught meat	_____

Part B

What chapters might contain information about the following subjects? There may be more than one.

Sample B		Indian Cooking	(7, 14) _____
(2, 6)	1.	Buffalo	_____
(11, 12, 13)	2.	Indian battles	_____
(9, 10, 14)	3.	Influences of the white man	_____
(3, 4, 5)	4.	Activities Indians enjoyed	_____
(6, 7, 8)	5.	Life in Indian village	_____
(1, 3)	6.	Beginnings of Indian civilization	_____
(9, 11)	7.	Wagon trains crossing the plains	_____
(14)	8.	Present-day life	_____
(6, 7, 14)	9.	Raising Indian children	_____
(1, 6, 7, 8, 14)	10.	The clothing Indians wore	_____

INFORMATION LOCATION TEST   LEVEL II

Directions to the teacher:

This test contains two parts. For each part the student will need the sample index and a test sheet. Answers may be written on a separate answer sheet if desired. Work the samples with the class and check the answers. It is not necessary for the student to put down all the listings. Answers given in parentheses are indicative of the many possible answers. Other answers may be accepted if the reasoning is logical.

Directions to the children:

As you know, the index of a book can be very useful in helping us find information about subjects we are studying. (Show an index in a book, if necessary.) Today we have an exercise to do using a sample index. Look over the index for a few minutes. The exercise is in two parts, but both parts use the same index. Look at your paper at part A. The directions say, "On what pages would you find information about the following subject?" The sample item is "comets." Look in your index and then write in the blank space the pages that would be about comets. What are the pages? Yes, 30 and 31 are correct. We also can include page 48 because it is about a special comet, so it is additional information. Does everyone understand why we listed those pages? The rest of part A is the same. Now let's look at part B. The directions say, "List all the numbers of the different categories that might have information about the following topics." The sample item is "Ways to view the stars." Write the number of all the categories you think fit there. Not the page numbers but the numbers in front of the names.

Do the sample now and then we'll check it together. . . . What were the possible categories? Very good. You may begin now. Do part A and then part B. If you don't know an answer just leave it blank.

SAMPLE INDEX

1.	Apparent time, 56, 57	24.	Mean solar day, 88
2.	Asteroids, 4	25.	Mercury, 62, 83
3.	Astronomical unit, 118	26.	Meteors, 88, 89
		27.	Milky Way, 71–74
4.	Barred spiral galaxies, 92, 93	28.	Moon, 5, 21–25
		29.	motion, 20
5.	Calendar, 48, 49	30.	tides, 23
6.	Celestial sphere, 58		
7.	Comets, 30, 31	31.	Neptune, 66, 89
8.	Constellations, 32, 33–35		
9.	Cosmic rays, 53, 60–63	32.	Planetarium, 106–108
		33.	Planets, 62–69
10.	Distance measurement, 110–114	34.	Pluto, 67, 90
11.	parallax method, 110, 111		
12.	scale models, 114	35.	Radio scopes, 115
13.	Dwarf stars, 23, 32, 36	36.	Radio telescopes, 110–119
		37.	Reflecting telescope, 114, 117
14.	Earth, 4–6	38.	Relativity, 40–42
15.	age of, 17, 18		
16.	motions of, 19, 20	39.	Saturn, 64, 87
		40.	Shooting stars, 44
17.	Galaxies, 82–87, 89–93	41.	Solar day, 99
18.	Giant stars, 65	42.	Solar system, 62–80
19.	Gravitational force, 17–19	43.	Space, 31
		44.	Stars, 61–63
20.	Halley's Comet, 48	45.	brightness, 63
		46.	evolution, 61–62
21.	Jupiter, 63, 65, 82	47.	Sun, 4–8
22.	Lunar month, 125	48.	Telescopes, 99–104
23.	Mars, 64, 83		

INFORMATION LOCATION TEST

Name _____

Part A

On what pages would you find information about the following subjects?

Sample: Comets   *(30, 31, 48)*

1. Age of the earth _____ *(17, 18)*
2. The tides _____ *(23)*
3. Small stars _____ *(23, 32, 36)*
4. How stars began _____ *(61–62)*
5. How gravity works _____ *(17–19)*
6. The moon _____ *(5, 20, 21–25, 125)*
7. Measuring miles in space _____ *(110–114, 118)*
8. Sun _____ *(4–8, 62–80, 88, 99)*
9. Large stars _____ *(32, 33–35, 65, 71–74, 82–87, 89–93)*
10. Viewing displays about space _____ *(106–108)*

Part B

List all the numbers of the different categories that might have information about the following topics.

Sample: Ways to view the stars   *(35, 36, 37, 48)*

1. Our solar system   *(14, 17, 21, 23, 25, 31, 33, 34, 39, 41, 47)*
2. Falling bodies in space   *(7, 20, 26, 40)*
3. Keeping time in space   *(1, 5, 22, 24)*
4. Star clusters   *(4, 6, 8, 13, 17, 18, 27, 44)*
5. Making space charts   *(8, 10, 11, 13, 35)*
6. Radiation in space   *(9, 19, 37, 47)*
7. Cause of tides   *(19, 28, 29, 30)*
8. Instruments for astronomy   *(10, 35, 36, 37, 48)*
9. Revolving bodies in space   *(2, 28, 29)*
10. The theory of relativity   *(10, 11, 38)*

INFORMATION LOCATION TEST   LEVEL III

Directions to the teacher:

Each child will need a test sheet. References and directions are on the sheet and should be read orally by the teacher to ensure everyone's understanding. If students do not know some of the references listed, they should merely skip them. Students are not expected to list all categories mentioned as possible answers.

Directions to the children:

Today you have a sheet with a list of titles of reference books you can find at most libraries. The directions on your sheet read: "If you needed to make a report on the following topics, which of the books listed above might have the information you would want? List the numbers that are beside the book title only. You may be able to use more than one. If you don't know what some of the books are just skip them." Are there any questions? You may go right to work.

Library Reference Books

1. Atlas
2. Dictionary
3. Encyclopedias
4. Familiar Quotations
5. Fieldbook of Natural History
6. Handbook to Literature
7. International Maritime Dictionary
8. Psychological Review
9. Readers' Guide to Periodical Literature
10. Statesman's Yearbook
11. Statistical Abstract of the United States
12. Thesaurus
13. Who's Who in the United States
14. World Almanac
15. Yearbook on Human Rights

INFORMATION LOCATION TEST

Name _____

Directions

If you needed to make a report on the following topics, which of the books listed above might have the information you would want? List the numbers that are beside the book title only. You may be able to use more than one. If you don't know what some of the books are just skip them.

1. Report on a famous living author   (3, 6, 9, 13)
2. Report on a U.S. senator   (3, 9, 10, 13, 14)
3. Report on world farming conditions   (1, 3, 9, 11, 14)
4. English report on poetic language   (4, 6, 9, 12)
5. Science report on ecology   (3, 5, 9, 11, 14)
6. Health report on mental illness   (3, 8, 9, 11, 15)
7. Social studies report on the United Nations   (3, 9, 10, 15)
8. Social studies report on a famous admiral   (3, 4, 7, 9, 13)
9. English report on word origins   (2, 3, 4, 6, 7, 9, 12)
10. A science report on the use of rats in experiments   (3, 5, 8)

SUMMARY

"Learning to read" and "reading to learn" are integral facets of the child's education. Being aware of the study skills that the student lacks and teaching to these needs will help him immeasurably as he moves up through the school system.

Study Skills Check Sheet

Check (✓) if child
has sufficient skill
in this area

STUDENTS	Scanning Level	Comprehension		Alphabetizing			Phonetic Skills				Dictionary Definitions	Information Location										
		I	II	I	II	III	I	II	III	IV		I	II	III								

145

List levels attained or
% correct - whichever
is appropriate for
section.

Date Tested-

STUDENT'S SKILLS

Scanning:
   Level I - Paragraph Reached
       % Comprehension
   Level II - Paragraph Reached
       % Comprehension
Alphabetizing:
   Level I - Words in List %
   Level II - Difficulty Level
   Level III - Guide Words %
Phonetic Dictionary Skills:
   Level I - Matching %
   Level II - Spelling %
   Level III - Diacritical Marks %
   Level IV - Accent %
Dictionary Definitions %
Information Location Test
   Level I - Table of Contents - A %
       - B %
   Level II - Index - A %
       - B %
   Level III - Reference Books %

NINE

Attitudes and Appreciations in Reading Skills Development

The main thrust of this book so far has been the assessment of particular reading skills. These skills have been divided into components around which tests have been designed to discover the particular strengths and weaknesses of each student. This process is extremely important to promote efficient use of the teacher's time and to develop material appropriate to the actual functioning level of the student. But the components examined by these tests are still only part of the total system that we call reading. Along with these particular skills come other, more intangible reading components that are equally important but are much more difficult to define and assess. These additional components are attitudes and appreciations. They are made up of the feelings and experiences related to reading, to school, to home, and to the self that the student brings with him to the classroom. For all their elusive nature, they can make the difference between success and failure for the child.

From the time the child is born he is exposed to language. In the beginning this language is oral, and he gradually learns through imitation and practice how to communicate. Research suggests that the years up to age four and a half constitute a most critical period in the child's development of language. During this period some children learn to enjoy books. Being read to can be a highly reinforcing experience, since the child receives individual attention and is able to interact in a positive way with parents, older siblings, or other adults. These pleasant experiences stimulate his interest in books and at the same time increase his exposure to a variety of language patterns. He learns new words, new ideas, and new ways of expressing himself as he hears the time-honored stories. The youngster who responds "It is I" to the question "Who is there?" is probably imitating his favorite *Three Billy Goats Gruff* rather than his family's typical response to such a question. Parents, nursery school teachers, and others can do much to increase the young child's awareness and appreciation of reading by handling the language exposure inherent in these procedures carefully, enthusiastically, and with sensitivity to the child's interest and needs.

Children who have many reading materials in their environment and who are frequently read to can often be found reliving the experiences they associate with the pictures and words in a particular story without anyone's reading the book to them. Some children learn a book practically word for word after a number of readings. They will announce that you are reading a book incorrectly when you skip a word or two accidentally, even though they have no knowledge of reading or the reading process. Instead, they have memorized what they have heard from previous readings. This type of memorization may lead the child to develop many of the skills necessary for beginning the reading process, such as left-to-right progression and visual and auditory discrimination. Some children will even build a beginning sight vocabulary based on their repeated exposure to favorite stories. By the time the child reaches the first grade classroom he may have acquired some skill in reading through this procedure. Certainly his physical maturity, his language maturity, and his attitudes toward books will greatly affect the type of program the teacher must provide.

Not all children, naturally, will have had the exposure to books or the experiences that provide growth toward reading. If the child lacks these experiences his attitudes toward reading may be very different from that of the child who has enjoyed early reading contacts. For such children the teacher's approach and methods at the beginning will prove most critical to their future attitudes and appreciations. Success in the child's early exposure to books and reading in the classroom can provide him great encouragement to pursue the reading task further. If the kindergarten and first grade teachers are well oriented toward this problem the child stands a good chance of succeeding in reading. He will find, for example, that he can gain independence in reading more quickly when he is able to identify certain words that are printed in the book rather than waiting for someone else to read them to him. And so his interest and independence will be encouraged.

There is a close relationship between the early development of competencies and attitudes in reading and the mastering of the reading process. These attitudes may well affect the child throughout life and certainly through many years of exposure to reading instruction. The old bromide that "nothing succeeds like success" may be more true for the learning of the reading process than for any other school-related subject. Low achievers in reading may be among the most frustrated and confused children in our schools. They recognize that their reading abilities are less than those of their peers and see in a direct or indirect way that the adults around them believe they are not succeeding. Because reading is such a central skill in the learning process, the child's attitudes toward himself and toward the school are greatly affected by his feelings of success and failure in this area. And all too often, reading failure does mean school failure for the child. Because the failure syndrome has such profound effects on the child and his attitudes toward reading, providing experiences that will provide sufficient success for the child must receive considerable thought and attention from the classroom teacher.

There are two principal factors that affect a child's attitude toward his reading in the school setting. One is the reinforcement he gets both intrinsically from reading with enjoyment and extrinsically from the teacher, other adults, or his peer group during the reading process and its associated tasks. Second, the child's interest in the material will determine in part the amount of time and effort he will put into reading it. For example, if he finds that books are available in the classroom that are closely related to his real interests and the interests of those he admires, his reading time will cease to be time taken from something more fun and will become worthwhile in itself. It is well to remember that from the child's point of view the task of reading is secondary to the subject matter he reads. If he really likes the book or magazine he will attempt to read it even though the material may be too difficult by some grading standard.

As the elementary years progress and the child's confidence in his ability to master reading skills increases, both the pace and the variety of reading tasks required of him can increase. The critical factor here is not the grade level or the sophistication of his reading skills but his attitude toward learning to read and his sense of competence in acquiring new skills and encountering novel learning experiences. If he feels successful, if he feels he can do it, and if he is provided with interesting materials that stimulate his curiosity and enthusiasm, he will learn to read. To capitalize on the interests of the child in helping him learn in reading or in any subject seems fairly obvious to the teacher, as does providing experiences at his level of functioning so that he can feel successful. But just as his particular strengths and weaknesses may not be immediately evident, so his interests and attitudes take time to determine. Here again testing may help the teacher assess interests and attitudes more quickly, providing information that can be used to choose books and plan stimulating lessons.

TESTING ATTITUDES AND INTERESTS

How does the teacher effectively determine the child's attitudes and interests toward reading and the subjects likely to be encountered in reading instruction? First, she determines the degree to which he identifies with the reading process. This is done with a simple questionnaire. This direct approach involves asking questions about his feelings toward books and reading, the kinds of books he likes, and his favorite activities. For example, a large number of topics can be listed from which the child can select his favorites. The child rates each of these areas on a scale based on his likes and dislikes. The scale starts with such general topics as animals, cars, science fiction, and space and progresses to specific areas like minibikes, horses, dancing, and moon landings. These questions are provided in fill-in, yes-no, multiple choice, and ranking formats. Additional questions worded slightly differently can be given the child later to help the teacher clarify the earlier answers or to indicate changes in attitudes and interests.

Attitudes toward the subject apart from the reading task itself are explored in this approach. For example, a child's negative reaction to reading may be counteracted by a positive reaction to drama or arithmetic. This would suggest to the teacher that reading about arithmetic or drama could be a productive approach in skill development activities having to do with reading.

In cases where children's attitudes are more negative toward reading and books, a more indirect approach is sometimes fruit-ful. One such approach is an attitude survey in which the child indicates on a scale how well a series of adjectives that is provided describes his feelings about school, himself, and reading. This format was originally developed by Osgood and is called the semantic differential. It helps the teacher gain insight into the child's personality and the attitudes that affect his behavior in the reading instruction situation. Second, the child can be asked to perform a task such as reading a passage. He is then asked to respond to a questionnaire about the amount of information he has gained from the passage, the amount of time he took to gain this information, and how he felt about this particular reading task. The advantage of this approach is that the child is not abstracting from some nonspecific past experience in which he has read numerous passages but instead is responding to a specific, immediate reading task while it is fresh in his memory. An example of the second approach is presented in part 3 of the following attitude and interest survey.

In any of the above techniques, it is important for the teacher to approach the assessment of reading attitudes without thinking of blaming or punishing the child. Certainly the child who feels that his answers on a test will affect the teacher's or his parents' attitude toward him will be more anxious and inclined to give answers that will make him "look good" rather than tell how he really feels. Anxiety may affect the test results either positively or negatively, but its presence should be noted by the teacher. The child's feelings about tests as well as reading may be reflected in his behavior. If he appears unduly nervous or anxious, fidgets a great deal, stops and starts, and so on, the teacher should record this information for later examination.

ATTITUDE AND INTEREST SURVEY

Note:

This survey is in three parts and may be given whole or in part. It is to be presented to the student as an interest survey rather than a test for attiudes. Generally speaking, the first part is the most direct and the other two parts are less so. It is a good idea to circulate while the students are filling out the survey to answer questions and help with unknown words. Since this is not a test in the usual sense, questions should be answered and discussion allowed as necessary.

ATTITUDES AND APPRECIATIONS IN READING SKILLS DEVELOPMENT **149**

Part A

Directions to the teacher:

The child will need the survey sheet only. Give plenty of time to read the items and fill in the blanks. Help with spelling, etc. only if requested.

Directions to the children:

Today you have an interest survey to fill out. This will help me choose books and activities for the class that we will all enjoy. Read each question and answer it the best you can. In some places you are to mark your choices, in other places you must write things in, so if you have any questions while you are working just raise your hand. You may start now.

INTEREST SURVEY

Name _____

Directions:

Circle the answers to these questions.

1. Do you like to read?   Yes   No
2. Do you have a favorite book?   Yes   No
3. Have you ever read a book more than once?   Yes   No
4. Have you ever read a book one of your friends said was good?   Yes   No
5. Do you go to the library?   Yes   No
6. Do you ever ask the teacher or librarian for help if you are looking for a book?   Yes   No
7. Do you ever read a book instead of watching television?   Yes   No
8. Do you read a book if you have seen the movie or television program based on it?   Yes   No

Directions:

Write the answers to the next questions.

1. What is the name of your favorite book or story? _____.
2. Name any book you have read more than once. Write how many times next to it. _____
3. Write the name of a book you *didn't* like and why. _____

Directions:

Below is a list of different kinds of books and stories. Put a 1 by all of the types of books you like best and a 2 by the kinds you like next best. Put an X by those you don't like. You may mark as many as you would like to.

_____ Adventure		_____ Horse stories	
_____ Animal stories		_____ Humor	
_____ Hobby stories		_____ Fantasy	
_____ Biography		_____ History	
_____ Autobiography		_____ Geography	

———— Science	———— Fables and myths
———— Western stories	———— Art and music
———— Sports	———— Religion
———— Fairy tales	———— People of other lands
———— Poetry books	———— Newspaper
———— Mystery	———— Magazines
———— Motorcycles and minibikes	———— Comic books
———— Love and romance	———— Ghost stories
———— Science fiction	———— Family stories
———— Car magazines	———— Riddles and jokes

Directions:

Now do the same thing for the subjects you like and don't like in school.

———— Arithmetic	———— Music
———— Spelling	———— Art
———— Reading	———— Physical education
———— Writing stories	———— Health
———— Science	———— Book reports
———— Social studies	———— English

Part B

Directions to the teacher:

The pupils will need the interest survey sheet only. Since this is not a strict test, questions may be answered and help given as necessary.

Directions to the children:

In the first part of this interest survey you are to number the choices in the order you like them best. Look at the top of your sheet and you will see the numbers from 1 to 7. Put the number 1 by the subjects or activities you like the most. Then put the number 2 by all the ones you like quite a bit, and so on. Number 7 is what you dislike the most. You don't have to use all the numbers, only those that seem to express your feelings the best. In the second part circle the word that best describes your feelings about a particular subject. If you have any questions or need any help while you are working just raise your hand. You may start now.

Directions:

In this part of the survey you are to rank the choices in each group in the following way. Fill in every blank.

1. Like very much
2. Like quite a bit
3. Like a little bit
4. Have no feelings about
5. Dislike a little bit
6. Dislike quite a bit
7. Dislike very much

1. Subjects in school

_____ Arithmetic	_____ Music
_____ Spelling	_____ Art
_____ Reading	_____ Physical education
_____ Writing stories	_____ Health
_____ Science	_____ Book reports
_____ Social studies	_____ English

2. Activities outside of school

_____ Television	_____ Reading
_____ Movies	_____ Cooking
_____ Outdoor games	_____ Hobbies
_____ Watching sports	_____ Animals
_____ Hiking and camping	_____ Trips
_____ Fishing	_____ Car races
_____ Riding horses	_____ Slot car races
_____ Riding minibikes and motorcycles	_____ Being with friends

3. Things to read about

_____ Adventures	_____ Horse stories
_____ Animal stories	_____ Humor
_____ Hobby stories	_____ Fantasy
_____ Biography	_____ History
_____ Autobiography	_____ Geography
_____ Science	_____ Fables and myths
_____ Western stories	_____ Art and music
_____ Sports	_____ Religion
_____ Fairy tales	_____ People of other lands
_____ Poetry books	_____ Newspaper
_____ Mystery	_____ Magazines
_____ Motorcycles and minibikes	_____ Comic books
_____ Love and romance	_____ Ghost stories
_____ Science fiction	_____ Family stories
_____ Car magazines	_____ Riddles and jokes

Directions:

In the next part of this survey circle the adjectives that best describe your feelings. You may circle more than one.

1. School makes me feel

    happy   excited   sad   interested   bored

2. My reading is

    excellent   good   all right   not too good   very poor

3. Reading books and stories is
    fun   exciting   interesting   boring   bad

4. I think about myself as
    tall   good-looking   plain   happy   smart   short   sad
    dumb   good

5. Teachers are
    busy   helpful   hurried   funny

6. Other kids are
    fun   friends   enemies   dull   good readers   poor sports
    like me   different from me

Part C

Directions to the teacher:

The students will need the interest survey sheet only. Give help as needed and answer all questions, since this is not a strict testing situation.

Directions to the children:

The papers that you have today contain some passages from different stories. After you read the stories you will answer some questions. They are about how you felt when you read the story. You are to circle the word or words that describes how you felt. Are there any questions? If you have questions as you work just raise your hand and I will come help you. You may begin now.

INTEREST SURVEY

Name _____

Directions:

Read the following stories. After you read each story circle the words that describe how you felt when you were reading.

Story A

Mike and Jim ran to their horses quickly. They knew they were going to have to ride fast if they were going to beat the storm. The black clouds were piling up faster and faster. "Come on, Jim, hurry up!" Mike yelled. "We'll never make it at this rate." "I'm trying, Mike," Jim shouted back, "but there's something wrong with this cinch. I can't seem to get it tight."

1. This story sounds
    dull   interesting   exciting   scary   silly

2. I would like to
    forget it   burn it   read it   hear it

3. It makes me feel
    good   alive   interested   bored   sorry

4. The author is probably
    dumb   smart   a good writer   a poor writer

Interest Check Sheet – Types of Reading

Check interest areas.

STUDENTS	Adventure	Animal Stories	Hobby Stories	Biography	Auto-biography	Science	Western Stories	Sports	Fairy Tales	Poetry	Mystery	Minibikes	Love and Romance	Science Fiction	Cars	Horse Stories	Humor	Fantasy	History	Geography	Art + Music	Ghost Stories	Family Stories	Riddles and Jokes

Interest Check Sheet – Subjects in School

Check interest areas

STUDENTS

	Arithmetic	Spelling	Reading	Writing Stories	Science	Social Studies	Music	Art	Physical Ed.	Health	Book Reports	English								

155

Story B

I'd always wanted to be in a taffy pull, and at last I was going to get a chance. Mother had said there would be one at the next Scout meeting and tonight was the night. She was bringing the sugar and a big pan to melt the syrup in. I could hardly wait to rub the butter all over my hands and then pull the soft candy until it turned white and hard. What a mess! And what fun!

1. This story sounds

    dull   interesting   exciting   scary   silly   fun

2. I would like to

    forget it   burn it   read it   hear it

3. It makes me feel

    good   alive   interested   bored   sorry   mad

4. I think reading is

    dumb   smart   fun   dull   boring   good

Story C

Janey peered through the green leaves. She was sure she had heard a sound in the middle of the big bush. The sunlight filtered through the tall trees of the forest, as Janey strained to see what was inside. Then a small movement caught her eye. Yes, there it was, a small fawn curled in a heap in the protection of the green leaves. "Ohh!" said Janey with a sigh, "he's probably waiting for his mother."

1. This story sounds

    dull   interesting   exciting   silly   enjoyable

2. I would like to

    read it   hear it   see it on television   forget it

3. Books are

    hard   easy   good   bad   interesting   boring

4. I am

    a good reader   a poor reader   an average reader   not a reader

BUILDING LITERARY APPRECIATION

Building on the child's interests and attempting to foster positive attitudes toward reading are worthy and important goals in the classroom. It has been found that one of the most effective and enjoyable ways to accomplish this is through the frequent use of literature in the reading and language arts program. Everyone enjoys a good story, regardless of age, and children seem to delight in identifying with their favorite story book characters. In addition, the richness of language expression greatly increases the child's repertoire of vocabulary and language patterns.

There are at least three principal avenues for building literary appreciation in the classroom, and they should all be included in a well-rounded program. The first is the teacher's frequent oral reading of passages designed to stimulate interest. This should be done regularly at odd moments. Poems, short stories, chapters from a book, or short excerpts are all appropriate. This can be done with small groups of children or the entire class but should be for relatively short periods of time. High-interest, fast-moving material related to the interests and age level of the audience are the best choices. Children can gain great appreciation of books and stories, poetry, and plays in this way. Even children who have read a story frequently enjoy hearing it again in oral form. The appreciation of great literature through this method with a teacher who is able to read well aloud is a highly motivating activity. Children who have heard a story will frequently ask for a chance to reread it independently so that they can reexperience it.

Oral reading also stimulates language experiences of all kinds in the classroom. It can stimulate the child's imagination, for example, which in turn can lead to creative writing and oral expression. Plays and puppet shows can grow from such stimulation. Oral reading can also help the child gain a feeling for an author's style as a means of starting to develop his own style of expression. The opportunity to discuss and compare story format and style is of great importance in helping him become aware of the nuances of language.

Another method of building literary appreciation is through language experience. In this approach the child reads his own stories and those of his friends. These stories may be based on individual or classroom experiences or may be modeled on a favorite story—"The Three Bears" may become "The Three Horses," or "Angus and the Ducks" may become "Skippy and the Chickens." In this way children learn much about the development of generative language. Frequently an individual has high interest in the language of the peer group, and so it has intrinsic attention value and motivation for him. This experience then stimulates an individual's own oral expression. A class newspaper, a chart story, or an individually generated story that is typed and distributed to the class can "turn the group on."

The third method of developing literary appreciation is through frequent exposure to the school or public library. By frequent and well-planned activity, children develop skill in using the library and an awareness of its vast resources. An early library habit can last the child all his life.

TESTS FOR INTERPRETATION AND INFERENTIAL READING SKILLS

Children who have extensive exposure to the language and style of good literature can develop many sophisticated reading skills. Through analogy, simile, metaphor, alliteration, and the like, authors add depth to the reader's understanding. The multiple meanings or the various shades of meaning of a given word or phrase not only add information to the passage from the reader's point of view but help him gain insight into the author's motives. A reader who has become sensitive to such techniques can utilize his own imagination and creative abilities to expand the actions and to generalize from the information provided. The enjoyment of fiction can also be greatly enhanced by encouraging children to anticipate the outcome of a passage and to predict the coming events and the actions of characters. A variety of activities for the extension of stories in time and location can be a great asset in the development of skill in interpretation and drawing inferences.

Tests can tap some of these skills and aid the teacher in planning further literary experiences for her class. Interpretation through word analysis is the basis of the first test in this area. In level I the student is asked to choose the best word of several to fit into a particular sentence. Various shades of meaning and alliterative techniques are employed.

Example: Soft silent shores and _____ _____ sand gleam sweetly in the summer sun.
(1) white
(2) silver
(3) sea
(4) packed

Synonyms and antonyms are explored in level II. The child is given a word and must decide what word in a sentence or passage it could replace. He must also decide if the meaning would be the same or opposite.

Key word: furious

           1   2   3   4   5
Sentence: The angry man sat down
    6
quickly.
Which word could be changed to the key word? 1 2 3 4 5 6
The meaning would be the _____ same _____ opposite
The child circles the appropriate answers.

In level III the ability to recognize words and phrases expressing the same or similar meanings is tested. In a given passage the child must find the words or phrases which do this.

Example: The pale moon shone in ghostly white. Its wan light was barely perceptible.

The child writes all the possible similar expressions. Answers: pale, ghostly, white, wan, barely perceptible.

The second test looks at interpretation and inference based on literary passages. In level I the student reads a passage and picks the best one-sentence interpretation in a multiple-choice format. In level II, he must decide what event or idea will follow from the passage given from a list of possible choices. In this test poetry will be used as well as prose, and ideas, moods, and feelings are interpreted as well as actual events.

LITERARY INTERPRETATION—WORD ANALYSIS TEST   LEVEL I

Directions to the teacher:

The student will need a test sheet. A separate answer sheet may be used if desired. Since literary interpretation is often fairly subtle, the "best" answer for a given passage is marked and only that answer is to be accepted even though there are other possibilities. Complete the samples with the group and check.

Directions to the children:

In the worksheet you have today, there are a number of sentences with words missing. After each sentence there are several possible answers. All of the answers may fit into the sentence but only one is the "best" one, the one that makes the sentence sound right. Look at sample A. We'll do it together. ————, read the sentence, please. What are our choices? Which one do you think is the "best" choice? Why does the word "mat" fit best? Right! It rhymes and it's something to sit on. Do sample B on your own. . . . Which answer did you choose as best? "Buttered" is right because it starts with "B" and has the same pattern as the old "Peter Piper picked a peck of pickled peppers." "Buttered biscuit" is the same pattern as "pickled peppers." Are there any questions? Do the rest on your own.

Name ————————————

Sample A

The cat in the hat sat on the ___(2)___ .
  1. chair
  2. mat
  3. rat
  4. couch

Sample B

Billy Button bought a ___(3)___ biscuit.
  1. baker's
  2. tasty
  3. buttered
  4. pickled

1. I scream, you scream, we all scream for ___(2)___ .
   1. pancakes
   2. ice cream
   3. peaches and cream
   4. coffee with cream

2. I hear the groan and moan of a dying man. His time is fleeing ___(4)___ .
   1. quickly
   2. furious
   3. soon
   4. fast

3. Come softly, lovely lady, and lay your ___(1)___ in mine.
   1. hand
   2. glove
   3. head
   4. heart

4. Soft silent shores and ___(2)___ sand gleam sweetly in the summer sun.
   1. white
   2. silver
   3. sea
   4. packed

5. The ___(3)___ sound made me shudder with dread as though the ghosts were warning me.
   1. whining
   2. crying
   3. wailing
   4. witching

6. "How dare you, sir?" the angry voice ___(2)___ .
   1. declared
   2. demanded
   3. decried
   4. said

7. Come, lovely child, and lift your lilting face to light. The world belongs to ___(4)___ .
   1. day
   2. you
   3. everyone
   4. loveliness

8. The sun is shooting wide its crimson ___(2)___ and still the child dreams.
   1. path
   2. glow
   3. way
   4. color

9. The shy shepherd herded his little ___(4)___ along the crooked path.
   1. group
   2. herd
   3. friends
   4. flock

10. Green grows the grass and ___(2)___ in the gracious air.
    1. grateful
    2. graceful
    3. flowers
    4. gruesome

Directions to the teacher:

The students will need the test sheet and a separate answer sheet, if desired. There will be one "best" answer for each sentence. If some students are unsure of the meaning of "opposite" do some extra explanation, possibly on the blackboard, before the main section of the test is begun. Complete the sample and check.

Directions to the children:

The worksheet you are going to do today is a little tricky. Look at the sample on your page. First you will see a key word. What is that word? . . . Right. Under that is a sentence. Who can read it? . . . Notice that each word in the sentence has a number over it. Now the question asks, "Which word could be changed to the key word—1, 2, 3, 4, 5, or 6? Is there a word in the sentence that you could substitute "furious" for? Right, "angry." What is the number above "angry"? Two is correct, so you would circle the number 2 to show that that is the word you could change. Now, the next sentence asks if the meaning of the sentence with the new word in it would be the same as before or the opposite. What would it be? Yes, since "furious" means the same as "angry" the meaning would be the same. Circle the word "same." Try sample B by yourself and then stop so we can check it. . . . All right, What is the key word? Who can read the sentence? Which word can be changed? Right! What is the meaning of the sentence now, the same or the opposite? Very good! Are there any questions? Do the rest of the questions on your own.

Name _____

Sample A

   Key word: furious

Sentence: The angry man sat down quickly.

Circle the answers:

   Which word could be changed to the key word?

   1   2   3   4   5   6

Meaning: same   opposite.

Sample B

   Key word: quiet

Sentence: The dogs next door are very noisy.

Circle the answer:

   Word to change: 1   2   3   4   5   6   7

Meaning: same   opposite.

1. Key word: ugly
    Sentence: The girl was truly lovely.
    (5, opp.)   Word to change: 1 2 3 4 5
    Meaning: same   opposite

2. Key word: barely
    Sentence: The food was abundantly spread.
    (4, opp.)   Word to change: 1 2 3 4 5
    Meaning: same   opposite

3. Key word: asset
    Sentence: Intelligence is definitely an advantage.
    (5, same)   Word to change: 1 2 3 4 5
    Meaning: same   opposite

4. Key word: possibly
    Sentence: Evidently we are going to leave soon.
    (1, opp.)   Word to change: 1 2 3 4 5 6 7
    Meaning: same   opposite

5. Key word: vigorous
    Sentence: The enormous boxer was very healthy.
    (6, same)   Word to change: 1 2 3 4 5 6
    Meaning: same   opposite

6. Key word: thrilling
    Sentence: The exciting race was almost finished when we arrived.
    (2, same)   Word to change: 1 2 3 4 5 6 7 8 9
    Meaning: same   opposite

7. Key word: chunky
    Sentence: The short stocky man was no match for the huge fighter.
    (3, same)   Word to change: 1 2 3 4 5 6 7 8 9 10 11
    Meaning: same   opposite

8. Key word: calm
    Sentence: She was obviously aggravated as she stood before the judge.
    (4, opp.)   Word to change: 1 2 3 4 5 6 7 8 9 10
    Meaning: same   opposite

9. Key word: interested
    Sentence: She made reference to the actor in an off-hand sort of way.
    (9, opp.)   Word to change: 1 2 3 4 5 6 7 8 9 10 11 12
    Meaning: same   opposite

10. Key word: quantity
    Sentence: The young girl passed out a multitude of copies of the song.
    (7, same)   Word to change: 1 2 3 4 5 6 7 8 9 10 11 12
    Meaning: same   opposite

Directions to the teacher:

Each child will need a test sheet and an answer sheet, if desired. The child is not necessarily expected to find all the similar expressions in a particular passage. Complete the samples with the class and answer any questions before beginning. If a child is unable to do the second sample, you may want to discontinue the test for that child.

Directions to the children:

In today's activity you are asked to do something a little different. Each sentence or group of sentences has several words in it that mean the same thing or almost the same thing. You are to find the words and write their numbers on the empty line after the sentence. Look at sample A. _____, read it please. Which words mean the same or almost the same thing? Yes, "squirmed" and "wiggled." How about "frisky"? It means "lively," doesn't it, but not necessarily "squirming," so we would not include it. What numbers would you write, then? Four and 6 are correct. Try sample B yourself and then we will check it. . . . All right, which words mean the same thing in this sentence? Yes, "hurry" and "speed" or "speed up." You can put 8 and 9 down because the two words together are one idea. The answers would be 1 and then you can put 8 dash 9 (write on board) to show these two words go together as one idea. Are there any questions? You may do the rest on your own.

Name _____

Sample A

    The frisky puppy squirmed and wiggled as she held him.   (4, 6)

Sample B

    "Hurry, Jimmy," Mother said. "We need to speed up if we are to get there on time."   (1, 8–9)

1. The world is full of wondrous things both marvelous and rare.   (6, 9)

2. She looked very old and tired. Her aged hands were trembling slightly. (4, 8)

3. The small birds darted here and dashed there in a frenzied hurry.   (4, 7)

4. The winding road twisted and turned in front of us.   (2, 4, 6)

5. The child was quite happy. Her gay laugh and delighted chatter could be heard by all.   (5, 7, 10)

6. The rain streams down this window and as it falls and runs it makes patterns and pictures with its trickles.   (3, 10, 12, 20)

7. Thank you for your help. I know you will serve and support us whenever you can be of assistance.   (5, 10, 12, 19)

8. She begged and implored but her master ignored her requests. He would accept no entreaties.   (2, 4, 10, 15)

9. The pale moon shone in ghostly white. Its wan light was barely perceptible. (2, 6, 7, 9, 12, 13)

10. The knight was considered bold and daring. Tales of his adventurous and fearless nature supported this brave picture.   (5, 7, 11, 13, 17)

LITERARY INTERPRETATION AND INFERENTIAL MEANINGS
LEVEL I

Directions to the teacher:

The student will need a test sheet. A separate answer sheet may be used if desired. Since this test concerns itself with literary interpretation, there may be more than one logical interpretation or inference from a particular passage.* However, only one "best" answer is marked. It is up to the individual teacher to decide if she wants to accept other alternatives. Complete the sample and check with students.

Directions to the children:

Today we have a worksheet that contains portions of stories, poems, and essays from various books. After each passage there are several statements that explain or interpret what the writing is about. Several may appear correct, but only one would be considered the "best" for that passage. Look at the sample and read it to yourself for a moment, then we'll do it together. . . . Who would like to read it for us? What are the possible interpretations of this description? _____
_____, read them please. Which do you think is correct? Yes, 2 is the best answer. Why did you choose it? How could you tell that there had been a big storm? On your answer sheet write your name. Then write "sample" and "2." Write the number of the passage and then the number that indicates the best answer for each item on your paper. Are there any questions? You may begin now.

Name _____

Sample

In a moment, all was again hushed. Dead silence succeeded the bellow of thunder, the roar of the wind, the rush of the waters, the moaning of the beasts, the screaming of the birds.
1. The animals were frightened.
2. A storm had passed.
3. The countryside was quiet.
4. We walked in the rain.

---

1. Success in every art, whatever may be the natural talent, is always the reward of industry and pains.
   1. Artists can be successful.
   2. It is important to have talent.

(3)   3. To succeed one must work hard.
   4. Life is full of pain.

2. Here rests his head upon the lap of earth.
   A youth to fortune and to fame unknown.
   1. The young man is poor.
   2. The young man is sleeping.

(4)   3. The young man is famous.
   4. The young man is dead.

3. The first general direction that should be given to the speaker is, that he should stand erect and firm, and in that posture that gives an expanded chest.

*All passages are taken from William H. McGuffey, *McGuffey's Sixth Eclectic Reader* (New York and Cincinnati: Winthrop B. Smith & Co., 1857).

1. You can breathe better if you stand straight.
2. When giving a speech you should stand straight.
(2)
3. Speakers should not breathe when talking.
4. Stand on both feet firmly when talking.

4. Below even this spacious grotto, there seemed another cavern, down which I ventured, and descended about fifty paces, by means of a rope.
1. The fun of mountain climbing.
2. Exploring a mountain.
(3)
3. Exploring a cave.
4. Using a climbing rope.

5. Alas! The white man's ax had been there. The tree that he had planted was dead; and the vine, which had leaped so vigorously from branch to branch, now yellow and withering, was falling to the ground. A deep groan burst from the heart of the Indian. For thirty years, he had watched that oak, with its twining tendrils. They were the only things left in the wide world for him to love, and they were gone.
1. The Indian is lonely and alone.
2. The white men are cruel.
(1)
3. The time of the Indian has passed.
4. Trees take a long time to grow.

6. There is a melancholy music in autumn. The leaves float sadly about with a look of peculiar desolation, waving capriciously in the wind, and falling with a just audible sound, that is a very sigh.
1. Leaves fall in autumn.
2. The wind blows in autumn.
(4)
3. Leaves make music when they fall.
4. Autumn is a sad time of year.

7. We will give the names of our fearless race
To each bright river whose course we trace;
We will leave our memory with mounts and floods
For the path of our daring, in boundless woods
1. Explorers name rivers.
2. Pioneers are going to a new land.
(2)
3. They are going on a trip.
4. The woods are dangerous.

8. On new year's night, an old man stood at his window, and looked, with a glance of fearful despair, up to the immovable, unfading heaven, and down upon the still, pure white earth, on which no one was now so joyless and sleepless as he.
1. The old man is celebrating.
2. The old man is unhappy.
(2)
3. The old man can't sleep.
4. It is snowing.

9. He woke, to die mid flame and smoke,
And shout, and groan and saber-stroke,
And death-shots falling thick and fast
As lightning from the mountain cloud.

(1)
1. The soldier died in battle.
2. There was a big fire.
3. There was a storm.
4. The soldier was asleep.

10. What rebellious thoughts of the cool river and some shady bathing place, kept tempting and urging that sturdy boy, who, with his shirt collar unbuttoned, and flung back as far as it could go, sat fanning his flushed face with a spelling book.
1. It is a hot day.
2. The boy doesn't like spelling.
(4)
3. The boy is lazy.
4. The boy would like to leave school.

LITERARY INTERPRETATION AND INFERENTIAL MEANINGS TEST
LEVEL II

Directions to the teacher:

The student will need a test sheet. A separate answer sheet may be used if desired. As with level I there is usually one "best" answer, but others may be accepted if the teacher wishes. Complete sample and check with students.

Directions to the children:

On our worksheet for today we have some parts of poems, stories, and essays. For each one you will try to decide what will happen next, either in an actual event or in a person's thoughts or feelings. Read the sample on your page and then we will do it together. . . . Who can read it for us? What are the possible answers? Which answer is correct? How did you decide they were going to fight? On your answer sheet put your name, then write "sample" and the number of the answer. What number should that be? Good! Do the same for the rest of the items. You may start now.

Name ——————————

Sample

They were both unarmed, and, stretching their limbs like men preparing for a desperate struggle, they planted their feet firmly on the ground, compressed their lips, knit their dark brows, and fixing fierce and watchful eyes on each other, stood there, prepared for the onset.
1. The men will run away.
2. The men will die.
(3)
3. The men will fight.
4. The men will turn to stone.

1. Meanwhile the south wind rose, and with black wings
Wide hovering: And now, the thickened sky
Like a dark ceiling stood.
1. It is going to rain.
2. It is going to be windy.
(1)
3. Birds are going to fly.
4. Clouds are gathering.

2. The sale began. After some paintings and engravings had been disposed of, Samuel's was exhibited. "Who bids three dollars? Who bids?" the auctioneer cried. The artist listened eagerly, but none answered. He thought to himself . . .
   1. "My work is no good."
   2. "The people are laughing at me."
   3. "Can I sell my work?"
   4. "No one will buy my picture."

(3)

3. "Away, away, o'er the foaming main!"
   This was the free and joyous strain—
   "There are clearer skies than ours afar;
   We will shape our course by a brighter star."
   1. The men will go on a trip.
   2. The people will go on a voyage.
   3. A storm is coming.
   4. The men are having a dream.

(2)

4. The tide and wind were so favorable, that the ship was able to come at once to the pier. It was thronged with people and there were repeated cheerings interchanged between shore and ship as friends happened to recognize each other.
   1. The mood of the meeting will be sad.
   2. The mood of the meeting will be reserved.
   3. The mood of the meeting will be interested.
   4. The mood of the meeting will be excited.

(4)

5. After we had landed on the island, we walked about four miles, through the midst of beautiful plains. At length we came to a little hill, on the side of which yawned a most horrid cavern which, by its gloom, at first struck us with terror. Recovering from the first surprise, however, we entered boldly.
   1. The men will find a bear in the cave.
   2. The cave will fall on them.
   3. The men will explore the cave.
   4. The men will become frightened and run away.

(3)

6. The few remaining trees, clothed in the fantastic mourning of autumn; the long line of heavy clouds melting away before the evening sun, and the distant mountains, seen through the blue mist of departing twilight, alone remained as he had seen them in his boyhood. All things spoke a sad language to the heart of the desolate Indian. "The pale face may like it, but an Indian cannot die here in peace," he cried.
   1. The Indian will die.
   2. The Indian will kill the white men.
   3. The Indian will put up his tepee.
   4. The Indian will leave this sad place.

(4)

7. But there is something in the thunder's voice, that makes me tremble like a child. I have tried to overcome this unmanly weakness but at the first low moaning of the distant cloud, my heart shrinks and dies within me. I am . . .

1. going to die of heart failure.
2. going to stay in the house till the storm passes.
(2) 3. going to run and hide.
4. going to put my head under the pillow.

8. Macpherson himself fell backward, his body hanging partly over the rock. A fragment gave way beneath him and he sank further, till catching with a desperate effort at the solid stone above, he . . .
   1. regained his footing.
   2. fell down the canyon.
(1) 3. yelled for help.
   4. gave a sigh of relief.

9. Oh Sailor-boy! Sailor-boy! never again
   Shall home, love, or kindred, thy wishes repay;
   Unbless'd and unhonor'd, down deep in the main,
   Full many a score fathom, thy frame shall decay.
   1. The sailor is going to battle.
   2. The sailor is having a dream.
(3) 3. The sailor is dead.
   4. The sailor is going home.

10. The pleasant rain! The pleasant rain!
    It hath pass'd above the earth.
    I see the smile of the opening cloud,
    Like the parted lips of mirth.
    1. It is going to rain.
    2. The flowers and grass will grow.
(2) 3. The sky will laugh.
    4. We will need umbrellas.

SUMMARY

In this chapter we have attempted to describe those skills in the reading area related to the affective domain. Certainly attitudes, appreciations, and skills in literary works are a significant part of the mature reader's repertoire of skills.

The tests in this section should give the teacher some insight into the extent of the child's exposure to literary form and analysis and the attitudes and interests he brings with him to the classroom. These can form the platform on which to build an effective literary skills program.

Check Sheet – Literary Interpretation

% Correct

STUDENTS	Word Analysis		Inference of Passages																	
	I	II	I	II	III															

Teacher's Guide to the Use
of Informal Reading Inventories

At the beginning of every year the teacher is faced with a new challenge and perhaps a new threat: "Where do I begin?" This is a common feeling and most appropriate to the season. The old answer "Begin at the beginning" doesn't quite fit, since we don't always know what the "beginning" is for a particular student. And that, of course, is our clue. We can start by finding out what that beginning point is for each student. And to do that, we must begin with a comprehensive testing program that will enable us to determine where to begin.

INITIATING THE READING
TESTING PROGRAM

Beginning the year with relaxed, get-acquainted activities interspersed with specific informal tests can prove a valuable and effective start for the teacher and students. This is especially so if it is made clear that the purpose of the testing is to help the teacher discover what the student needs to learn. Testing should not be approached as a threat or punishment for the student, as is too often the case with both testing and grading. Instead it is a means of getting help. Tests can help the teacher select material that is appropriate, and they can help the student by revealing his strengths and weak-

nesses. In many cases an open, accurate accounting to the child of the results of the tests can help him to gain insight into his own problems and develop an increased awareness of the purposes of instruction in the areas where he has difficulty. To discover these difficulties, however, we need to employ a careful sequence of tests.

In initiating a test sequence it is important to identify the general capabilities of the individual before starting to develop a profile on the specific skills that he possesses. It is especially important to get a general idea of the child's broad reading skills and his potential reading levels so that the level of difficulty of the tests that he will face can be adjusted to his present capabilities. For example, a child who is already doing some reading generally needs to receive both oral and silent reading tests so that he can be given specific skills tests at a level that will neither frustrate him unduly nor waste time and resources. As a general rule, it is advisable to initiate a specific skills testing program at a level that is well within the child's independent reading level. For some children, this may be as much as two or three levels below his instructional reading level.

The specific skill tests to be used following the general testing battery should be suggested by weaknesses indicated in the general tests. It may even be wise to give some children a few items from each of the specific skills tests to provide a check on the information gathered in the general testing sessions regarding their strengths in different areas. For example, an upper elementary pupil occasionally fails to master some basic skill such as identifying the names of the letters of the alphabet. If each teacher assumes that the child learned the skill before he came to her, his weaknesses can slip by undetected year after year.

Tests should be administered in increasingly difficult stages until the child reaches a level of performance that allows a careful analysis of the test results and clearly suggests instructional needs. In other words, we don't know what to teach until the child misses something. Correct responses may tell us what we don't have to teach that child, but mistakes and an analysis of their types tell us how to plan our instructional time more effectively.

Still, it is well to remember that one bit of data on a child is insufficient to construct an instructional plan for him. Plans should be based on repeated measures of a given skill with different types of tests to ensure that the information being gathered is, in fact, a reflection of his ability in the specific skill rather than a function of his emotional responses to a particular test-taking situation.

SUGGESTED GROUPS OF TESTS

Each of the tests that have been described in this volume are cross-level inventories—that is, they are designed for a variety of competence levels. Since not only do the various students in a class differ in skill level, but also a particular student may vary greatly from one subject or skill to another, the usefulness of a particular inventory with a given individual is best determined by the teacher. The guide that follows is only an approximate indicator of the tests that may be appropriate for various levels of functioning. If the reading process is viewed as a whole consisting of increasingly complex skills that develop both independently and in interaction with each other, the concept of levels of functioning becomes more meaningful than that of specific grades or years in school.

Tests should be selected from the following groupings or from other available tests as they seem appropriate to the particular class or child being tested.

Prereading and beginning level reading tests

1. Tests for auditory and visual discrimination and memory
2. Tests for learning modalities (where indicated in special circumstances, particularly tactile discrimination)
3. Generative language tests, including test of echoics
4. Listening comprehension
5. Following directions
6. Alphabet recognition and generation tests
7. Letter-sound correspondence

Primary level reading tests

1. Oral and silent reading paragraphs
2. Letter-sound correspondence
3. Listening comprehension
4. Blending
5. Syllabication
6. Following directions
7. Alphabetizing skills

Intermediate level reading tests

1. Oral and silent reading paragraphs
2. Blending
3. Syllabication
4. Structural analysis
5. Alphabetizing skills
6. Dictionary skills tests, including phonetics and definitions
7. Following directions
8. Attitude and interest inventory

Upper level reading tests

1. Oral and silent reading paragraphs
2. Following directions
3. Structural analysis
4. Dictionary skills: phonetics and definitions
5. Study skills, including information location and scanning
6. Literary inference and multiple meanings
7. Attitude and interest

Again it must be emphasized that the general test pattern at the beginning of the year will vary greatly from child to child and from group to group. Some children may need to "hurry backwards," especially if their oral reading paragraphs indicate needs in many skill areas. The least complex level in which the child needs instruction is most important. For example, if the child seems to be having trouble with letter names, his auditory discrimination should be tested before his knowledge of letter-sound correspondence. He must learn to hear differences in sounds before he can hope to learn to associate a particular sound with a particular letter. Since children with reading problems often have multiple difficulties we must be sure to test at a level that will get back to the basic components of a particular skill.

A teacher will often want to test an area again later in the school year for such purposes as to gather data on the effectiveness of the instruction pattern. If a weakness was originally discovered in the area of basic vocabulary development and it now seems to be corrected, it is important to determine whether it really is. In most instances this determination requires an alternate form of the test that was given at the outset of the school year.

An alternate form usually consists of the same type of test with the items modified or rearranged slightly. This is often referred to as a pretest-posttest pattern. It is important that both tests be similar in format to provide an equivalence in the testing situation. Alternate forms also guard against the memory effect that appears when the same form is repeated. A child may remember the specific items he missed and choose the right answers on an identical retest not because he has learned them but because he can remember the isolated example from the pretest.

Retesting before the end of the school year on specific curriculum areas can assist the teacher in determining the effectiveness of the program and may also suggest procedural changes to improve instructional efficiency. However, a caution related to retesting must be mentioned. Tests can cause a child anxiety that may be harmful in later learning situations. This is particularly true if the child knows he has numerous difficulties that prevent his achieving at the level of his expectations. If given too frequently, tests can create such tension that they will not measure performance accurately nor permit an atmosphere in which the child can grow at an optimum rate.

FLEXIBILITY OF TESTING PROCEDURES

Increasing the number of items in the sample tests will benefit teachers who want more information on an individual's strengths or weaknesses in a particular skill area. For instance, a particular inventory may contain eight or ten items related to medial vowels but may not identify to the teacher's satisfaction the particular vowels with which the child needs help. Five or ten more items in the same format may pinpoint the problem. This addition could include specific items in the area where the child's class performance has indicated weakness. Language experience stories, for example, can be one source which will give the teacher clues to the child's vocabulary problems. It may be well to consider these words as the basis of the additional inventory items. Partial testing is suggested for teachers who wish only to survey the skill areas where more complete inventories are provided. By carefully selecting items from each of the appropriate inventories, the teacher can increase the number of skills tested and decrease the time necessary for testing.

GROUPING FOR TEST ADMINISTRATION

Obviously, the larger the group to be tested and the fewer the number of tests administered, the more efficiently the relevant data can be gathered.

Administration must be carefully planned to ensure that the children clearly understand the directions of the test and are following them properly. A group that is too large for the type of test being given does not provide true efficiency. Many of the informal inventories suggested here can be administered to an entire class of normal children at one sitting. Caution is advised, however, since many classes include children whose understanding of oral and written directions and whose ability to work independently for an extended period of time is not as great as those of their peers. Testing in large groups may not be valid for such individuals, and adjustments in procedures will be required. The teacher may find it necessary to place these children in a smaller group and test them under close supervision while the rest of the class works on a test that can be completed independently. The tape recorder with sets of earphones also offers numerous possibilities in testing. Many simple group tests can be administered with it, especially if the teacher checks to see that sample items are done correctly. The machine is also helpful for the inevitable student who enters the class after the beginning-of-the-year testing program is completed.

Some informal inventories in this volume must be individually administered. These naturally include all tests that require an oral response from the child. Such tests can best be given during a recess period, after school hours, or during times when others in the class are working with different projects. A quiet corner reserved for the purpose will help these tests go smoothly.

ANALYZING AND INTERPRETING TEST RESULTS

Test results should be recorded on group check sheets and profile sheets such as the ones included in the various chapters or appendices. The individual profile will also be useful in determining a child's specific skill needs at a glance. After this information is recorded, the teacher may want to keep a file of some kind so that she can easily use her results. Often a loose-leaf notebook with the names of individual children is helpful.

The analysis of the results of tests and informal inventories requires skill. If the teacher observes that a child performs a given reading task effectively in class, she should expect his performance on a valid test of this skill to reflect this ability. In the same way a child with a day-to-day problem in a particular area should perform similarly on informal inventories. Discrepancies in test results and on-going performance should be followed up by the teacher until she is satisfied she has a valid assessment of the child's skills. If the test results support the teacher's initial guesses, then she should share this information with the child. A child needs to become aware of what skills he needs. He also needs opportunities to work in the skill areas indicated by the inventories, and he needs information regarding his progress. The reinforcement and motivation that should arise from the analysis of the skill profile become an important part of a child's sense of prog-

ress. Seeing for himself where he stands at different points in time helps him set goals for himself and increases his feeling of success. Success is the teacher's most powerful ally.

Another word of caution is in order. Test results are highly personal information. Making them public through such devices as posting a class profile on a bulletin board may be devastating for one child who has a low score. Confidentiality is particularly important for grades and the evaluation of the results of end-of-the-year tests. Positive attitudes and feelings of self-confidence that have been carefully developed during the entire year can be destroyed if this sensitive area is overlooked.

CONSTRUCTION OF INFORMAL READING INVENTORIES

Since every class and every child is unique, there will probably come a time when the teacher decides she needs a new test to meet special needs. The construction of informal inventories is relatively easy if a few general principles are followed.

Format

Each test item should have a format that is simple and easily understood. If the child can see clearly and intuitively the nature of the task, then he is free to concentrate his energies on the test items themselves without being unduly concerned with the mechanics of taking the test. For instance, a child who is asked to use a separate answer sheet before he really understands the correspondence of the test item and the number on the answer sheet may record many answers incorrectly or spend too much time figuring out where the answer goes.

In the primary levels, in general, the kind of test in which the answers are placed on the same sheet as the test item are recommended. Intermediate level children generally can be expected to respond to the tests on separate answer sheets without getting test item numbers or other administrative features confused.

The number of steps and the degree of abstraction required of the test taker should gradually increase. A child should start each test with items he can answer easily and quickly to allow him to establish a solid base in a particular skill area.

We must also consider the child's emotional reaction to the test itself. If he feels that he can succeed in the testing situation, that he can answer some of the items correctly, he is more likely to have a positive attitude toward the entire procedure and is more likely to try to do his best.

It cannot be denied, however, that from a diagnostic point of view the more difficult the items, the more value to the teacher and the reading specialist, since they give us a more accurate picture of the child's needs. A balance between difficult items and "emotional support" items must be found.

Directions

It is important in the development of informal inventories to consider the role of the directions to the student. They should always be behaviorally oriented. This means that each step should require an action that can be monitored by the teacher or another person. Thus the test administrator gains immediate feedback regarding the effectiveness of the directions, since the child must demonstrate that he understands his instructions by doing what the instructions ask. Instead of telling the primary grade child to look at the word "directions," for example, the teacher can ask him to "point to or underline the word. The directions should be clear and simply stated. There should be a minimum of words, and each word should clearly state what is to be done. Simple words should be used, not words the children may not know. An example of clear directions, behaviorly oriented, is: "Put your pencil on the number 1. Now put your pencil on the picture of the cat beside the number 1. Now put your pencil on the word cat. Underline it. Now find the word 'cat' in the box. Underline it. Do not underline any other word in the box."

Test administrators should keep in mind that many children may not know left from right. It is better to label a column with something clearly recognizable to the child, such as a picture of an animal or a star, than to ask the child to look at the left-hand side of the page.

Finally, the directions should contain performance samples. They give the child an opportunity to perform the required task in a practice situation and let the test administrator make sure that the child clearly understands the task by observing him perform it correctly.

Administration

From the point of view of the test administrator, it is important that a test be easy to give. Testing can be unnecessarily time consuming, both in administration and scoring, unless careful thought is given to the form of the test items and answer sheets and to the steps necessary to arrive at a valid score for each student. A child in the upper grades may express his ideas best in an essay format. Yet scoring techniques for essay material are not as efficient as a true-false or multiple-choice format, even though the latter techniques do not yield the amount of information in a reading comprehension test that essays do. This is not to say that essay tests are not appropriate, but rather that there are many times when other types of tests will serve the purpose of the teacher with a substantial saving of time in administration and scoring.

Expense is also a factor to be considered. The limited resources at the command of most teachers require that time and materials for tests be used in the most efficient manner possible. An example of low-cost test techniques is utilization of separate answer sheets for intermediate and upper level students wherever possible. This is true in informal inventories as well as standardized tests. The reuse of the test forms with long paragraphs or other involved items may save the teacher many hours of retyping and mimeographing.

Following these simple guidelines in format, directions, and administration should make it possible to create or rework tests as needed to get specific and appropriate information regarding student needs.

SUMMARY

The utilization of informal reading inventories and the analysis of their results should bring a teacher closer knowledge of the instructional needs of the children in her class. It must be emphasized that a flexible approach is necessary in testing reading skills. It is vital that each teacher constantly assess the effectiveness of her instruction. Data are necessary to make the modifications that will make her program more relevant to the students' needs. The tests should give the teacher the maximum amount of information on the degree to which she needs to or has been able to improve the children's skills, and this information can be among the most rewarding in the teaching profession. It is only in the constant evaluation of an individual's skills that one can come up with a valid and realistic approach to the teaching of reading.

Bibliography

SELECTED TESTS

ALPERT, HARVEY, et al. *Sequential Tests of Educational Progress: Reading.* Princeton, N.J.: Cooperative Test Division, Educational Testing Service, 1956–1957.

BENDER, LAURETTA. *Bender Visual Motor Gestalt Test.* New York: American Orthopsychiatric Association, 1938–1946.

Botel Reading Inventory. Chicago: Follett Publishing Co., 1961; *Guide to the Botel Reading Inventory.* Chicago: Follett Publishing Company, 1961.

DOLCH, E. W. *The Basic Sight Word Test.* Champaign, Ill.: Garrand Press, 1942.

DURRELL, DONALD D. *Durrell Analysis of Reading Difficulty.* New York: Harcourt Brace Jovanovich, 1937–1955. For grades 1–6; one form for individual administration in grades 1–6; time 30–90 minutes.

EARLY, MARGARET J., et al. *Sequential Tests of Educational Progress: Listening.* Princeton, N.J.: Cooperative Test Division, Educational Testing Service, 1956–1957. For grades 13–14, level 1; for grades 10–12, level 2; for grades 7–9, level 3; for grades 4–6, level 4; forms A and B yield one overall score.

FROSTIG, MARIANNE, D. W. LEFEVER, and J. WHITTLESEY. "A Developmental Test of Visual Perception for Evaluating Normal and Neurologically Handicapped Children." *Perceptual and Motor Skills,* 12:383–94, June 1961.

GATES, ARTHUR I. *Gates Reading Diagnostic Tests.* Rev. ed. New York: Teachers College Press, 1953. For grades 1–8, time 60–90 minutes.

GRAY, WILLIAM S. *Gray Oral Reading Test.* Indianapolis: Bobbs-Merrill Co., 1963.

JASTAK, JOSEPH. *Wide Range Achievement Test and Manual,* 1946.

JOHNSON, ELEANOR. "Phonics Inventories." Published periodically in *My Weekly Reader.*

LAIRD, J. T., and C. B. FULLER. "Minnesota Percepto-diagnostic Test." *Journal of Clinical Psychology,* 1962–1963.

McCARTHY, J. J. "The Illinois Test of Psycholinguistic Abilities: An Approach to Differential Diagnosis." *American Journal of Mental Deficiency,* 65:399–412, November 1961.

McCULLOUGH, CONSTANCE M. *McCullough Word Analysis Test.* Boston: Ginn & Co., 1962.

SMITH, NILA BANTON. *Graded Selections for Informal Reading: Diagnosis for Grades 1 through 3.* New York: New York University Press, 1959.

175

WEPMAN, J. M. *Wepman Auditory Discrimination Test.* Chicago: Language Research Associates, 1958.

WINTER HAVEN LIONS CLUB. *Perceptual Forms Test, Ages 6–8.5.* Winter Haven, Fla.: Winter Haven Lions Research Foundation, Inc., 1955–1963.

SELECTED READINGS

AUSTIN, MARY C., *et al. Reading Evaluation.* New York: Ronald Press Co., 1961.

BARRETT, T. "Taxonomy of Cognitive and Affective Dimensions of Reading Comprehension." Unpublished paper, University of Wisconsin, 1967.

BETTS, EMMETT A. *Foundations of Reading Instruction.* New York: American Book Co., 1957.

BLOOMER, RICHARD H. "The Cloze Procedure as a Remedial Reading Exercise." *Journal of Developmental Reading,* 5: (spring 1962), 173–81.

BOND, GUY L. "Diagnostic Teaching in the Classroom." In *Reading Diagnosis and Evaluation, 1968 Proceedings,* edited by Dorothy DeBoer, vol. 13, part 4. Newark, Del.: International Reading Association, 1970.

BORMUTH, JOHN R. "Mean Word Depth as a Predictor of Comprehension Difficulty." *California Journal of Educational Research,* 15:226–31, November 1964.

BURNETT, RICHARD W. "The Diagnostic Proficiency of Teachers of Reading." *Reading Teacher,* 16:229–34, January 1963.

BUROS, OSCAR K., ed. *The Sixth Mental Measurements Yearbook.* Highland Park, N.J.: Gryphon Press, 1965.

COHN, STELLA M., and JACK COHN. *Teaching the Retarded Reader: A Guide for Teachers, Reading Specialists, and Supervisors.* New York: Odyssey Press, 1967.

COLEMAN, J. H., and ANN JUNGBLUT. "Children's Likes and Dislikes about What They Read." *Journal of Educational Research,* 44:221–28, February 1961.

CULHANE, J. "Cloze Procedures and Comprehension." *Reading Teacher,* 21:227–34, 1967.

De HIRSCH, KATRINA, JEANNETTE JANSY, and W. S. LANGFORD. *Predicting Reading Failure.* New York: Harper & Row, 1966.

DELLA-PIANA, GABRIEL, BETTY JO JENSEN, and EVERETT MURDOCK. "New Directions for Informal Reading Assessment." In *Reading Difficulties: Diagnosis, Correction, and Remediation,* edited by William K. Durr. Newark, Del.: International Reading Association, 1970, pp. 127–32.

DURR, WILLIAM K., ed. *Reading Difficulties: Diagnosis, Correction, and Remediation.* Newark, Del.: International Reading Association, 1970.

DYKSTRA, ROBERT. "Auditory Discrimination Abilities and Beginning Reading Achievement." *Reading Research Quarterly,* 1:5–34, spring 1966.

FREIDMAN, MILES, *et al.* "Readiness and Instruction: Individual Diagnosis and Treatment." In *Critical Issues in Research Related to Disadvantaged Children,* edited by Edith Grothberg. Princeton, N.J.: Educational Testing Service, 1969.

GLASS, GERALD G. "Students' Misconceptions Concerning Their Reading." *Reading Teacher,* 12:765–68, May 1968.

GOLDHAMMER, ROBERT. *Clinical Supervision.* New York: Holt, Rinehart & Winston, 1969.

HAFNER, LAWRENCE E., and HAYDEN B. JOLLY. *Patterns of Teaching Reading in the Elementary School.* New York: Macmillan, 1972.

HARRIS, LARRY A. and CARL B. SMITH. *Reading Instruction Through Diagnostic Teaching.* New York: Holt, Rinehart & Winston, 1972.

HOCKER, MARY ELSA. "A Case-Study Approach to Reading Problems." *Reading Teacher,* 21:541–43, March 1968.

HOLMES, JACK A. "Personality Characteristics of the Disabled Reader." *Journal of Developmental Reading,* 4:111–22, winter 1961.

HUNT, J. T. "Selecting a High School Reading Test." *High School Journal*, 39:49–52, October 1955.

HUNTER, MADELINE. "When the Teacher Diagnoses Learning." *Educational Leadership*, 23:545–49, April 1966.

JOHNSON, MARJORIE SEDDON, and ROY A. KRESS. *Informal Reading Inventories*. Reading Aids Series. Newark, Del.: International Reading Association, 1965.

KASS, CORRINE E. "Psycholinguistic Disabilities of Children with Reading Problems." *Exceptional Children*, 32:533–39, April 1966.

KIRK, SAMUEL A. *The Diagnosis and Remediation of Psycholinguistic Disabilities*. Urbana: University of Illinois Press, 1966.

KOTTMEYER, WILLIAM. *Teacher's Guide for Remedial Reading*. New York: McGraw-Hill Book Co., 1959.

LARRICK, NANCY. *A Teacher's Guide to Children's Books*. Columbus, Ohio: Charles E. Merrill Books, 1960.

MAYER, ROBERT W. "A Study of the STEP Reading, SCAT and WISC Tests, and School Grades." *Reading Teacher*, 12:117–42, December 1958.

McCRACKEN, ROBERT A. "Standardized Reading Tests and Informal Reading Inventories." *Education*, 82:366–69, February 1962.

MILLER, WILMA H. *The First R: Elementary Reading Today*. New York: Holt, Rinehart & Winston, 1972.

PORTERFIELD, O. V. and H. F. SCHLICHTING. "Peer Status and Reading Achievement." *Journal of Educational Research*, 54:292–97, April 1961.

POWELL, WILLIAM R., and COLIN G. DUNKELD. "Validity of the IRS Reading Levels." *Elementary English* (in press).

ROSWELL, FLORENCE, and GLADYS NATCHEZ. *Reading Disability: Diagnosis and Treatment*. New York: Basic Books, 1964.

RUSSELL, DAVID. *Listening Aids through the Grades: One Hundred Ninety Listening Activities*. New York: Teachers College Press, 1970.

SHELDON, WILLIAM D. "Teacher Must Diagnose." *Education*, 78:545–46, May 1958.

SPACHE, GEORGE D. "Integrating Diagnosis with Remediation in Reading." *Elementary School Journal*, 56:18–26, September 1955.

STRANG, RUTH, CONSTANCE M. McCULLOUGH, and ARTHUR E. TRAXLER. *The Improvement of Reading*. 4th ed. New York: McGraw-Hill Book Co., 1967.

———. "Evaluation of Development in and through Reading." In *Development in and through Reading: Sixtieth Yearbook of the National Society for the Study of Education*. Chicago: University of Chicago Press, 1961, pp. 376–97.

TYLER, FRED, ed. *Individualizing Instruction; Sixty-first Yearbook of the National Society for the Study of Education*. Chicago: University of Chicago Press, 1962.

WILSON, ROBERT M. *Diagnostic and Remedial Reading for Classroom and Clinic*. Columbus, Ohio: Charles E. Merrill Books, 1967.

ZINTZ, MILES V. *The Reading Process: The Teacher and the Learner*. Dubuque, Iowa: William C. Brown Co., 1970.

Appendix I
Tests

Subject	Reference Page	Appendix Page
Visual Discrimination Test Level I	23	181-182
Visual Discrimination Test Level II	23	183-184
Visual Discrimination Test Level III	22	185
Visual Memory	25	187-188
Silent Reading Paragraphs	108	189-190
Alphabetizing Test	130	191-192
Sample Pronunciation Key	132	193
Phonetic Dictionary Skills	137	195-196
Information Location Tests	140-143	197-202

A. ◁	⬡	○	△	▭
B. ▯	△	▭	▭	○
1. ⬡	▷	⬡	▱	⬡
2. O	O	L	M	K
3. N	N	A	M	V
4. B	C	B	D	B
5. J	ſ	J	L	J
6. W	A	V	M	W

#					Target
7.	P	D	B	q	P
8.	c	C	c	d	c
9.	n	m	h	n	m
10.	b	g	p	d	b
11.	-	r	n	r	r
12.	z	s	8	z	s
13.	w	w	m	ε	3
14.	9	8	e	9	6

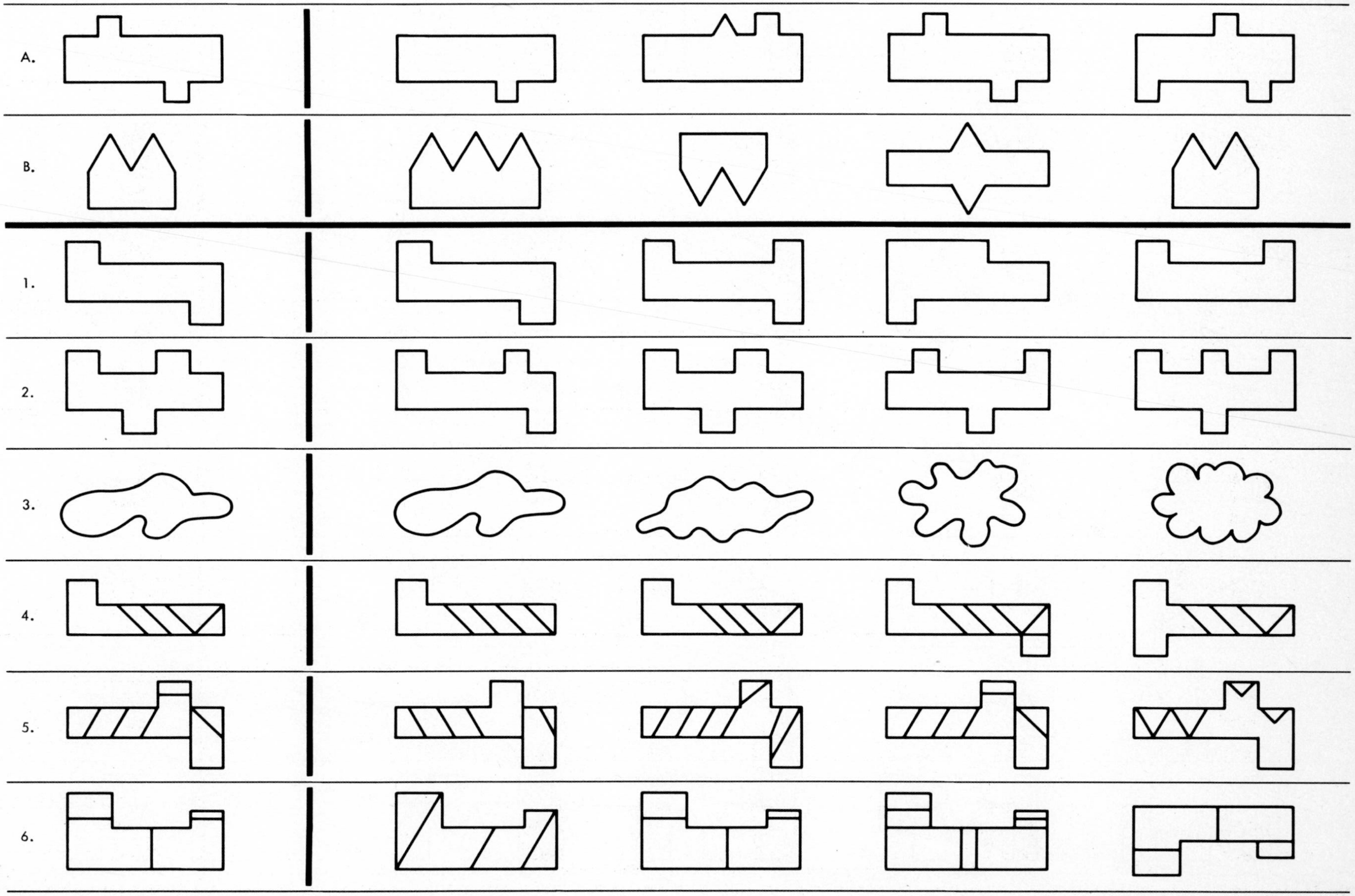
A.
B.
1.
2.
3.
4.
5.
6.

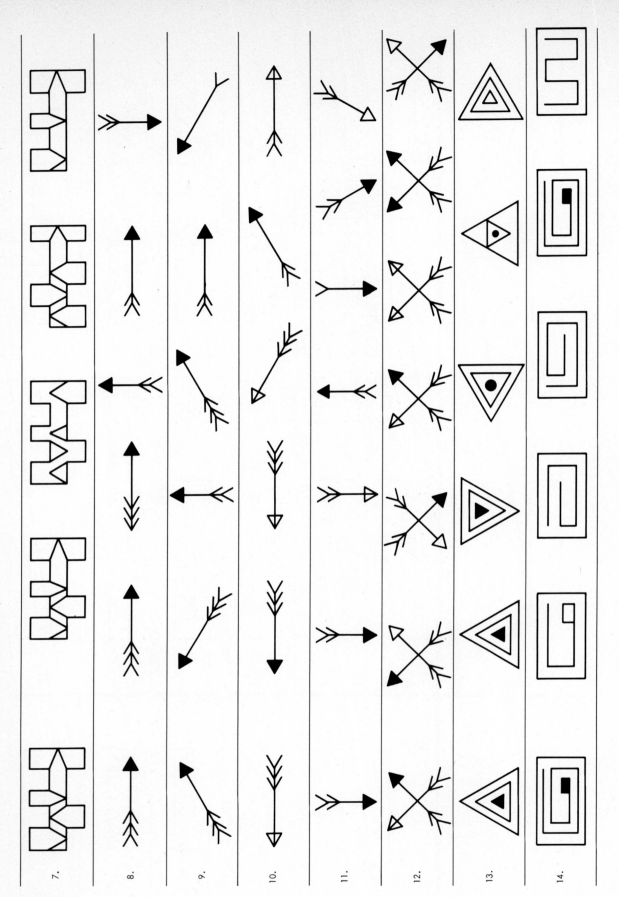

VISUAL DISCRIMINATION   LEVEL III

		bq	pd	bd	bp
A.	bp	gn	ph	bh	gh
B.	mnn	mnm	nmm	mnn	nnm
1.	gh	gn	ph	bh	gh
2.	ssb	bss	ssd	ssb	sbs
3.	sob	sbo	bos	sod	sob
4.	not	ton	not	hot	toh
5.	bad	bab	bad	bob	dad
6.	ursq	urqs	usrq	nrsq	ursq
7.	today	tobay	tadoy	dayto	today
8.	brwiltz	drwiltz	brwildz	brwiltz	brwlitz
9.	roughen	roughen	ruoghen	nouphen	roughon
10.	moisten	noisten	moistem	moisten	miosten
11.	dentally	dentally	dentally	bentally	dentaly
12.	beautiful	beuatiful	deautiful	becutiful	beautiful
13.	lbingpiomy	lbingpinoy	ldingpiomy	lbingpiomy	lbinggiony
14.	discriminate	disoriminate	discriminate	discriminate	biscriminate

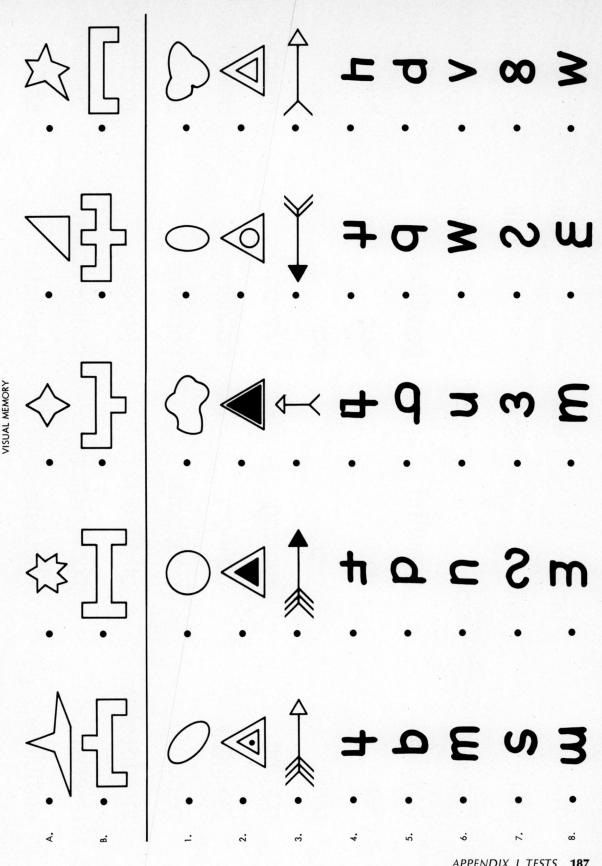

9.	awb	baw	wba	wab	abw
10.	still	stlll	stil	tsill	stlll
11.	hppo	hipo	oppih	hippo	hipop
12.	baeutiful	beautiful	beautiful	beauitful	beautiufl
13.	bob	dod	dod	dob	bod
14.	pen	gen	gen	pon	peu
15.	nurring	running	running	runniug	rnuuing
16.	ballingry	balinpry	bolingry	bolingry	ballinger
17.	populate	podubate	popalete	popalete	poplte
18.	straddecker	strodbecker	strodbecker	strobdek	srodbecker
19.	reservation	conservation	conservation	consternation	concerning
20.	stimulate	stipulate	sintillate	sintillate	sintilap

"Look at these  , Mother," said Jane.

"I like the red . I like the blue 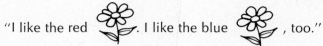 , too."

"Yes, Jane. They are pretty," said Mother.

"Come in the  , Jane.

We will look at the  later."

"Can I help, Mother?" said Jane.

"Yes, you can help. Come in the ."

Memory

1. What does Jane like?

2. What colors are the flowers?

Inference

3. Where are Mother and Jane?

Interpretation

4. Why does Jane want to help?

ALPHABETIZING TEST

Name _____

Guide words are found at the top of each page in the dictionary and in some other reference books. They are repeating the first word on the page and the last word on the page. They can help us find words more quickly.

They look like this:

Sample:

baby	89	ball

Circle the words that would be on this page:

baffle   back   break   baa   banner

Part A

1.

trump	950	trust

trumpet   trunk   tree   truss   truly

2.

veterinarian	1258	vicar

vexed   vestry   vial   vibrate   victory

3.

fortune	325	foul

fortunate   fossil   forward   foster   found

4.

blind	98	blood

block   blend   bleed   bliss   blot

5.

untold	1303	up

unto   untrue   untangle   untouchable   unwritten

Name _____

Part B

instantaneously	615	insufficient
insufficiently	616	integrator
integrity	617	intensive
knavery	652	knock
knockabout	653	k.o.

The following word would be on what page?

Sample: intense   ___617___

1.   instrument   _____   _____

2.   knob   _____   _____

3.   intact   _____   _____

4.   integral   _____   _____

5.   instinct   _____   _____

6.   knuckle   _____   _____

7.   insurance   _____   _____

8.   knell   _____   _____

9.   insufficiency   _____   _____

10.   intelligence   _____   _____

11.   knot   _____   _____

12.   intended   _____   _____

SAMPLE PRONUNCIATION KEY

Accent Markings:

(/), as in mother (mŭth′ ər), is used to mark primary accent or stress; the syllable preceding it is pronounced with greater emphasis than other syllables in the word. Silent letters are not included. Upside-down letters stand for unaccented syllables: ə ; ɐ in alone, ə in system.

ă	act, mat	ō	own, no
ā	able, cake	ô	corn, call
ã	dare, chair	oi	oil, boy
ä	car, calm	ou	cloud, out
b	back, tub	p	pat, top
ch	choose, beach	r	rake, cry
d	do, Ted	s	saw, hiss
ĕ	shell, set	sh	shoe, push
ē	knee, equal	t	ten, pit
f	fit, farmer	th	thin, path
g	beg, get	th	then, breathe
h	hit, hat	ŭ	sun, love
hw	when, why	ū	cute, few
ĭ	chill, if	ũ	urge, bird
ī	rise, flight	u̇	pull, took
j	just, edge	ü	true, ooze
k	kept, cap	v	voice, live
l	low, all	w	west, way
m	mine, Tim	y	you, yes
n	on, now	z	zeal, those
ŏ	clock, hot	zh	vision, beige

Name _____

Directions:

Circle the phonetic spelling that stands for the underlined word.

Sample A

The night was very *quiet*.
a. kwĭt   b. kwī′ et

Sample B

You are very *definite* about the answer.
a. dĕf′ e nĭt   b. dĭ fī′ nt

===

1. *Whose* dog is that?
   a. hōz   b. hüz

2. A *whale* is a huge sea animal.
   a. hălb   b. hwāl

3. I would like to be an ice *skater*.
   a. skăt r′   b. skāt′ r

4. The blue *bird* is very pretty.
   a. bŭrd   b. brīd

5. Pour the water from the *pitcher*.
   a. pĭch′ r   b. pĭk′ch r

6. The *author* wrote many good books.
   a. ô′ther   b. ŭth′er

7. He has on one black *shoe* and one brown one.
   a. shō   b. shü

8. Please cancel the order.
   a. kăn sel′   b. kăn′s l

9. His job is *below* hers.
   a. bĭ lō′   b. bĕl′ō

10. Who is the main *character*?
    a. chăr′ ti   b. kăr′ĭk tr

Name _____

Sample A

The escaped _____ was frightened.

   a. con'vict   b. con vict'

Sample B

I know nothing about the _____.

   a. sub'ject   b. sub ject'

==

   1. We made good _____ in arithmetic.

         a. prog'ress   b. pro gress'

   2. The men were lost in the _____.

         a. dez'ert   b. de zurt'

   3. I bought a new _____ today.

         a. re kord'   b. rek' ərd

   4. There was a large pile of _____ by the curb.

         a. ref'us   b. re fuz'

   5. I received a watch for a _____.

         a. pre'sent   b. pre sent'

   6. He got a _____ to sell candy.

         a. per'mit   b. per mit'

   7. You must give me a _____.

         a. re'fund   b. re fund'

   8. Many _____ fought against the government.

         a. re bels'   b. re'bels

   9. I am _____ to stay here.

         a. kon'tent   b. kon tent'

  10. Will you _____ me home?

         a. kon'duct   b. kən duct'

SAMPLE TABLE OF CONTENTS

Chapter	Title	Page
1	Indians of Prehistory	8
2	Indian Horses	16
3	Sign Language and Picture Writing	23
4	Indian Sports and Pleasures	29
5	Indian Art	36
6	How an Indian Brave Lived	42
7	How an Indian Woman Lived	50
8	How the Medicine Men Lived	56
9	White Men Come to America	65
10	Early Treaties	75
11	Indian Massacres	85
12	On the Warpath	96
13	Custer's Last Stand	105
14	Indians Today	112
	Index	125

INFORMATION LOCATION TEST

Name _____

Part 1

Write the page number for the chapter that probably tells you about the following things.

Sample A   Animals of the Indians   _____(16)_____

  1.   Indian medicine   _____

  2.   A famous battle   _____

  3.   The earliest Indians   _____

  4.   Pictures by Indians   _____

  5.   Agreements signed with Indians   _____

  6.   How Indians live now   _____

  7.   Games Indians played   _____

  8.   Jobs of an Indian woman   _____

  9.   Ways Indians wrote things down   _____

10.   How a brave caught meat   _____

Part 2

What chapters might contain information about the following subjects? There may be more than one.

Sample B   Indian Cooking   _____(7, 14)_____

  1.   Buffalo   _____

  2.   Indian battles   _____

  3.   Influences of the white man   _____

  4.   Activities Indians enjoyed   _____

  5.   Life in Indian village   _____

  6.   Beginnings of Indian civilization   _____

  7.   Wagon trains crossing the plains   _____

  8.   Present-day life   _____

  9.   Raising Indian children   _____

10.   The clothing Indians wore   _____

SAMPLE INDEX

1. Apparent time, 56, 57

2. Asteroids, 4

3. Astronomical unit, 118

4. Barred spiral galaxies, 92, 93

5. Calendar, 48, 49

6. Celestial sphere, 58

7. Comets, 30, 31

8. Constellations, 32, 33–35

9. Cosmic rays, 53, 60—63

10. Distance measurement, 110–114

11. parallax method, 110, 111

12. scale models, 114

13. Dwarf stars, 23, 32, 36

14. Earth, 4–6

15. age of, 17, 18

16. motions of, 19, 20

17. Galaxies, 82–87, 89–93

18. Giant stars, 65

19. Gravitational force, 17–19

20. Halley's Comet, 48

21. Jupiter, 63, 65, 82

22. Lunar month, 125

23. Mars, 64, 83

24. Mean solar day, 88

25. Mercury, 62, 83

26. Meteors, 88, 89

27. Milky Way, 71–74

28. Moon, 5, 21–25

29. motion, 20

30. tides, 23

31. Neptune, 66, 89

32. Planetarium, 106–108

33. Planets, 62–69

34. Pluto, 67, 90

35. Radio scopes, 115

36. Radio telescope, 110–119

37. Reflecting telescope, 114, 117

38. Relativity, 40–42

39. Saturn, 64, 87

40. Shooting stars, 44

41. Solar day, 99

42. Solar system, 62–80

43. Space, 31

44. Stars, 61–63

45. brightness, 63

46. evolution, 61–62

47. Sun, 4–8

48. Telescopes, 99–104

Name _____

Part 1

On what pages would you find information about the following subjects?

Sample: Comets   (30, 31, 48)

1. Age of the earth _____

2. The tides _____

3. Small stars _____

4. How stars began _____

5. How gravity works _____

6. The moon _____

7. Measuring miles in space _____

8. Sun _____

9. Large stars _____

10. Viewing displays about space _____

Part 2

List all the numbers of the different categories that might have information about the following topics.

Sample: Ways to view the stars   (35, 36, 37, 48)

1. Our solar system

2. Falling bodies in space

3. Keeping time in space

4. Star clusters

5. Making space charts

6. Radiation in space

7. Cause of tides

8. Instruments for astronomy

9. Revolving bodies in space

10. The theory of relativity

Library Reference Books

1. Atlas

2. Dictionary

3. Encyclopedias

4. Familiar Quotations

5. Fieldbook of Natural History

6. Handbook to Literature

7. International Maritime Dictionary

8. Psychological Review

9. Reader's Guide to Periodical Literature

10. Statesman's Yearbook

11. Statistical Abstract of the United States

12. Thesaurus

13. Who's Who in the United States

14. World Almanac

15. Yearbook on Human Rights

INFORMATION LOCATION TEST

Name _____

Directions

If you needed to make a report on the following topics, which of the books listed above might have the information you would want? List the numbers that are beside the book title only. You may be able to use more than one. If you don't know what some of the books are just skip them.

1. Report on a famous living author

2. Report on a U.S. senator

3. Report on world farming conditions

4. English report on poetic language

5. Science report on ecology

6. Health report on mental illness

7. Social studies report on the United Nations

8. Social studies report on a famous admiral

9. English report on word origins

10. A science report on the use of rats in experiments

Appendix II
Answer Sheets

Subject	Reference Page	Appendix Page
Auditory Discrimination Test Answer Sheet	16	205
Generative Language Skills	40	207
Generative Language Skills	41	208
Generative Language Skills	42	209
Generative Language Skills	42	210
Generative Language Skills	43	211
Listening Comprehension Test Part 1A	47	212
Listening Comprehension Test Part 1B	49	213
Listening Comprehension Test Part 2	51	214
Listening Comprehension Test Part 3	53	215

NAME _____

A. 🙂 🙁

B. 🙂 🙁

1. 🙂 🙁

2. 🙂 🙁

3. 🙂 🙁

4. 🙂 🙁

5. 🙂 🙁

6. 🙂 🙁

7. 🙂 🙁

8. 🙂 🙁

9. 🙂 🙁

10. 🙂 🙁

11. 🙂 🙁

12. 🙂 🙁

13. 🙂 🙁

14. 🙂 🙁

15. 🙂 🙁

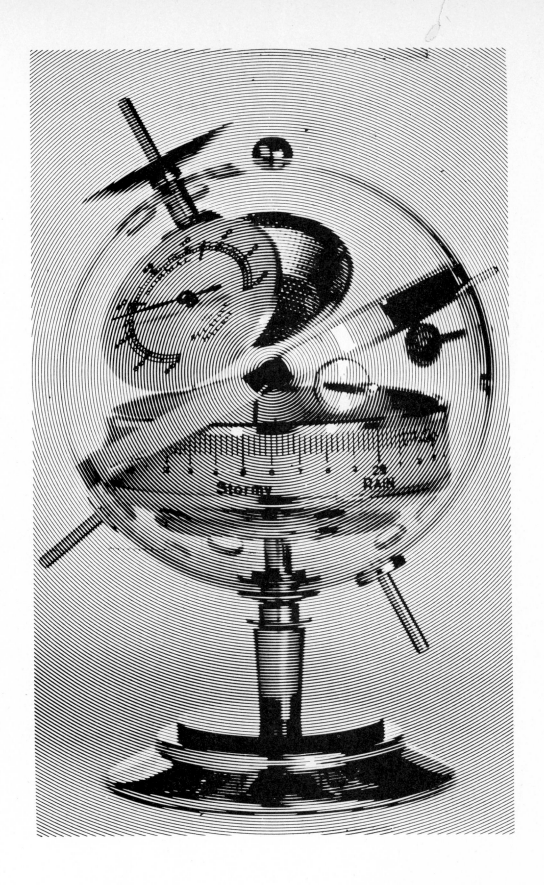

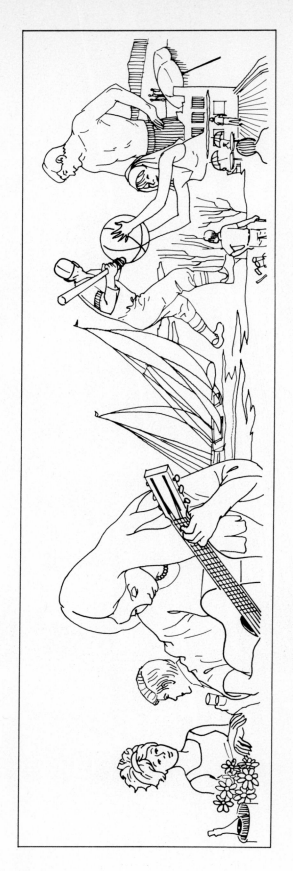

LISTENING COMPREHENSION TEST

PART I   SECTION A   CHILD'S ANSWER SHEET

NAME _____   GRADE _____

A.

1.

2.

3.

4.

5.

6.

7.

8.

9.

10.

CHILD'S ANSWER SHEET

Name ———————————   Grade ————————

Sample

      A.   The cat was: (1) little (2) white (3) grey.

      B.   The mouse was: (1) white (2) tiny (3) grey.

1.   The dog was: (1) old (2) gray (3) sleepy (4) soft.

2.   The cowhand was: (1) young (2) sleepy (3) tall (4) old.

3.   The person talking was: (1) eating (2) dreaming (3) yawning (4) hopping.

4.   The time of day is: (1) morning (2) afternoon (3) night (4) summer.

5.   The morning light is: (1) gray (2) white (3) hard (4) soft.

6.   The house was: (1) new (2) dirty (3) old (4) fancy.

7.   The man was: (1) young (2) tall (3) fast (4) jumpy.

8.   The stairs were: (1) steep (2) dusty (3) brick (4) stone.

9.   The children were: (1) quick (2) exhausted (3) happy (4) sitting.

10.   The dogs were: (1) running (2) chasing (3) jumping (4) exhausted.

11.   The ground was covered with: (1) grass (2) leaves (3) flowers (4) dogs.

12.   The room was: (1) deserted (2) lonely (3) intense (4) large.

13.   The men were: (1) talking (2) staring (3) sitting (4) drinking.

14.   The glasses were: (1) half full (2) half empty (3) completely full (4) completely empty.

15.   The men are going to: (1) sing (2) drink (3) part (4) join.

LISTENING COMPREHENSION TEST

Part 2   CHILD'S ANSWER SHEET

Name _____   Grade _____

Sample A

How would you describe Joe?

(1) lazy (2) careful (3) old (4) cruel

1. The horses were: (1) resting (2) playing (3) working.

2. They felt: (1) cross (2) hot (3) tired.

3. The children were: (1) noisy (2) frightened (3) angry (4) happy.

4. The man was: (1) angry (2) calm (3) hurried (4) gentle.

5. The time was: (1) evening (2) summer (3) morning (4) afternoon.

6. The cowhand had been: (1) working (2) sleeping (3) eating (4) rude.

7. The girl is: (1) sick (2) happy (3) sad (4) crazy.

8. The girl is probably: (1) lonely (2) busy (3) an actress (4) his mother.

9. The young man is probably: (1) a soldier (2) a photographer (3) her father (4) with the girl.

10. Jane thinks: (1) Jim can read (2) Jim is tall (3) Jim is kind (4) Jim is busy.

11. Jane wants Jim to: (1) read to her (2) help her understand (3) return her book (4) go to the library.

12. The ship is: (1) old and cracked (2) in a storm (3) on a cruise (4) falling apart.

13. The captain is: (1) abandoning the ship (2) radioing for help (3) putting the sailors to work (4) going to sleep.

14. The main message of this story is: (1) the coming of winter (2) how bugs are different from horses (3) how colorful the day was (4) the power and contrast in young life.

15. Young animals live: (1) only in pastures and under logs (2) in large numbers (3) only if they can run fast (4) in many different conditions.

Name _____   Grade _____

1. What does that sentence mean?
    _____ If you save money you will only get pennies.
    _____ If you save money you can be a coin collector.
    _____ If you save money it is like earning it.

2. What should the reader do according to that statement?
    _____ Live a long time.
    _____ Be careful and save the lives of others.
    _____ Realize that if he is careless he will endanger his life as
                    well as others.

3. The statement means;
    _____ You should learn to sew.
    _____ Fixing something right away will keep it from getting
                    worse.
    _____ In time things will get better.

4. This probably means;
    _____ Your cuts and bruises will get better.
    _____ We need to learn first aid.
    _____ We will forget about the things that have hurt us after
                    awhile.

5. This tells us;
    _____ If we do something right away it will work out better
                    for us.
    _____ Birds get up early.
    _____ Worms are good to eat.

6. What is likely to happen next?
    _____ ran away.
    _____ hit the tree again.
    _____ sharpened his ax.
    _____ yelled "timber."

7. What is likely to happen next?
    _____ stopped.
    _____ turned to ice.
    _____ melted.
    _____ caused a flood.

8. Days later he discovered;
    _____ he had poison oak.
    _____ he had a snake bite.
    _____ he was lost.
    _____ he was hungry.

9. They knew they would soon hear;
    _____ a horn.
    _____ yelling.
    _____ thunder.
    _____ a policeman.

10. All was quiet until Johnny yelled;
    _____ "I caught a fish."
    _____ "I'm sleepy."
    _____ "I want to go home."
    _____ "I see a pretty cloud."

Index

Index

A

Accuracy of oral language, test for, 42–43
Administration of tests, 173
Affixes, 57, 85
    tests for, 87–90
Alliteration, 157
Alphabet recognition and generation test, 57–60
Alphabetization skill, 119
    test for, 126–31, 189–90
Analogy, 157
Antonyms, 119, 157
Attitudes and appreciations, 147–68
    interest test and, 149–56
    literary appreciation and, 156–57
Auditory tests:
    for auditory discrimination, 12, 13–20
    for auditory memory, 22–23, 26–29

B

Bibliography, use of, 118
Blends of sounds, 57, 65, 77–81
    consonants and digraphs test and, 57, 73–75
    syllabication and, 81

C

Card catalog, use of, 119
Cloze test for silent reading, 106–7, 111–15
Comparisons, 57
Consonant sounds, 57, 61–62
    syllabication and, 81
    tests for, 71–75

Cultural background:
    language skills related to, 37
    reading attitudes and, 147–48

D

Definitions, dictionary, 119
    test for, 137–39
Diagnostic process:
    overview of, 1–5
    principles of, 2
Dictionary, use of, 119
    definitions skills test and, 137–39
    information location test and, 139, 143
    phonetic skills test and, 131–37, 193–94
Digraphs, 57, 61
    syllabication and, 81
    tests for, 65, 73–75
Diphthongs, 57
Directions for testing, 173
    following, 43–45

E

Echoic language skills test, 37–39
Encyclopedia, use of, 119
    information location test and, 139, 143
Environment:
    language skills related to, 37
    reading attitudes and, 147–48
Essay tests, 173
Evaluation, paragraph reading and, 105–6

219

F

Failure syndrome, reading ability and, 148
Footnotes, use of, 118
Format of tests, 172
Frustration level of reading, 95, 106, 169

G

Generative language test, 39–44
    See also Language skills
Graded Silent Reading Paragraphs test, 105–11
Grapheme, 56
Group tests, 4
Grouping of students, 171–72

I

Independent level of reading, 95, 106, 169
Index, use of, 118, 119
    information location test and, 139, 141–43,
        197–98
Individual instruction, need for, 1
Individual tests, 3–4
Inferential analysis:
    literary interpretation test and, 163–68
    of oral language test, 51–53
Inflectional endings, 57, 85
Information location tests, 139–46
    index test and, 139, 141–43, 197–98
    reference books tests and, 143–46, 199–200
    table of contents test and, 139–41, 195–96
Insertions, in oral reading, 95
Instructional level of reading, 95, 106, 169
Interests:
    attitude toward reading and, 148
    tests for, 149–56
Intermediate level tests, 170
Interpretation of oral language test, 49–50

K

Key words, recognition of, 93

L

Language skills:
    accuracy of oral language test, 42–43
    echoic test, 37–39
    following directions test, 43–44
    generative test, 39–44
    inferential analysis test, 51–53
    interpretation of oral language test, 49–50
    listening comprehension test, 45–49, 51,
        53–54
    quantity of oral language test, 41–42
Learning modalities test, 32–35
Letter-sound correspondence test, 61–81

Levels of reading, 95, 106, 169
Levels of testing, 170
Library use, literary appreciation and, 157
Listening comprehension test, 45–55, 213–15
    following directions and, 43–45
Literary appreciation, 119, 156–57
    inferential analysis test and, 163–68
    word analysis test and, 158–62

M

Metaphor, 157
Mixing of sounds, in oral reading, 94
Model of reading, 6–11

O

Omissions, in oral reading, 94
Oral language skills:
    generative tests and, 39–44
    inferential analysis test and, 51–53
    interpretation test and, 49–50
Oral reading, 1, 91–103
    compared with silent reading, 92, 104, 105
    individual tests of, 3
    limitations of, 92–93, 94
    literary appreciation and, 156–57
    problems of, 94–95
    quick assessment of, 94
    San Diego Quick Assessment of Reading
        Ability test and, 94, 95–97
    short paragraph test of, 94
    test of, 93–103
    uses of, 93

P

Paragraphs:
    in oral reading test, 94
    in silent reading test, 105–11, 187
Peer group relationships, oral reading and, 92
Perceptual discrimination, 12–36
    auditory discrimination tests and, 12, 13–20
    auditory memory test and, 22–23, 26–29
    individual profile sheet for, 36
    learning modalities test and, 32–35
    visual discrimination test and, 12–13, 20–21,
        183
    visual memory test and, 22–25
Phoneme, 56
Phonetic keys in dictionary, 119
    test for, 131–37, 193–94
Phonics and word analysis:
    alphabet recognition and generation test
        and, 57–60
    auditory discrimination and, 12
    letter-sound correspondence tests and,
        61–81
    structural analysis test and, 85–90
    syllabication test and, 81–84

Plurals, 57
    test for, 86–87
Poetry, oral reading and, 93
Prefixes, 57, 85
    test for, 87–90
Prereading level test, 170
Pretest-posttest pattern, 171
Primary level tests, 170
Program of testing, 169–74
    analyzing results of, 172
    construction of inventories and, 172–73
    flexibility of, 171
    grouping students for, 171–72
    groups of tests for, 170–71
    initiation of, 169–70
Pronunciation key, 191
Punctuation, oral reading and, 94

Q

Quantity of oral language, test for, 41–42
Quotations, use of, 118

R

Rate of reading, 93, 105, 106
Readers' Guide to Periodical Literature, 119
    information location test and, 143
Recall of information test, 48–49
Receptive skills, *see* Language skills
Reference books, information location test and,
    143–46, 199–200
Reference skills, *see* Study and reference skills
Refusal, in oral reading, 94, 95
Reinforcement, attitude toward reading and, 148
Repeating ability, test for, 37–39
Root words, 57
    identification test for, 85–86

S

San Diego Quick Assessment of Reading Ability,
    94, 95–97
Scanning:
    study skills and, 117–19
    test for, 119–26
Semantic differential testing, 149
Silent reading, 1
    cloze test for, 106–7, 111–15
    compared with oral reading, 92, 104, 105
    decoding and, 104–5
    flexibility of rate of, 106
    paragraph test and, 105–11, 187
    problems of, 94
    study skills and, 105
Simile, 157
Size of classes, 1, 171
Skills sequence, 6–8
Sound-symbol relationships, 56–57, 60, 61–81

Sources, use of in books, 118
Standardized tests, 3
Structural analysis of words, 57
    test of, 85–90
Study and reference skills:
    alphabetizing skills test and, 130–31
    definitions test and, 137–39
    information location test and, 139–46
    phonetics test and, 131–37
    scanning test and, 117–19, 119–26
    silent reading and, 105
    word information skills and, 119
Success feelings, reading ability and, 148
Suffixes, 57, 85
    test for, 87–90
Syllabication, 57
    rules for, 81
    test for, 81–84
Synonyms:
    in dictionary and thesaurus, 119
    use of, 105, 118, 157
Synthesis, paragraph reading and, 106

T

Table of contents, information location test and,
    139–41, 195–96
Tactile discrimination test, 13, 29–31
Teacher's guide to testing program, see Program
    of testing
Thesaurus, use of, 119
    information location test and, 139, 143
Translation, paragraph reading and, 105–6

U

Upper level tests, 170

V

Variety of oral language, test for, 40–41
Verb endings, 57
Visual test:
    for visual discrimination, 12–13, 20–21, 183
    for visual memory, 22–25
Vocabulary knowledge, 148
    beginning reading and, 37, 104
Vowel sounds, 57, 61, 65
    syllabication and, 81
    test for, 66–67, 77

W

Word calling, 92–93
Words:
    literary interpretation test and, 157–62
    structural analysis of, 57, 85–90
    See also Phonics and word analysis